Creating Happily Ever After

Creating Happily Ever After:

A Marriage Manual for What to Do After the Honeymoon is Over

Michelle E. Vásquez, MS, LPC

Copyright © 2011 Michelle E. Vásquez, MS, LPC.

All rights reserved. No portion of this book may be reproduced mechanically, electronically, or by any other means, including photocopying, without written permission of the publisher. It is illegal to copy this book, post it to a website, or distribute it by any other means without permission from the publisher.

First Edition

Cover design by Sam Desai, Jim Temple
Cover photograph by Michael Enis
Jacket copyrighting by Len Diamond
Author photograph by Mike Altshuler

Michelle E. Vásquez, MS, LPC
19051 Goldenwest St., Suite 106-410
Huntington Beach, CA 92648
714-717-5744

Email:	michelle@michellevasquez.com
Web sites:	http://trueloverelationshipcoaching.com
	http://askmichelleanything.com
Social media:	twitter.com/trueloveafter40
	http://profile.to/michellevasquez
	http://www.linkedin.com/in/michellevasquez

Limits of Liability and Disclaimer of Warranty
The author and publisher shall not be liable for your misuse of this material. This book is strictly for informational and educational purposes.

Warning – Disclaimer
The purpose of this book is to educate and entertain. The author and/or publisher do not guarantee that anyone following these techniques, suggestions, tips, ideas, or strategies will become successful. The author and/or publisher shall have neither liability nor responsibility to anyone with respect to any loss or damage caused, or alleged to be caused, directly or indirectly by the information contained in this book.

ISBN: 978-0-9834638-0-1

Cover photograph: Kylemore Castle was built by Mitchell Henry in 1868 for his wife and family after he had inherited a family fortune. Kylemore Abbey has been the home of the Benedictine Nuns since they purchased it in 1920. The nuns were formerly known in Belgium as the Dames of Ypres where they had their monastery and a school. With the outbreak of World War I and Ypres bombed, they returned to Ireland, their founding home. The nuns continued the tradition of a school and the cloistered life. The school closed in 2010 when vocations to the Order declined. Nuns still reside at the Abbey and steward the estate while continuing to live the cloistered life. They are still committed to education and sharing their liturgy and prayer with visitors to the Abbey.

What people are saying about Michelle, True Love Relationship Coaching, and *Creating Happily Ever After*:

"You certainly have helped me apply more completely the concepts of the rule of attraction, and maintain my sense of self-confidence in the face of what was at the time a seemingly insurmountable set of circumstances (being single looking for 'the one')."
Matt S., San Antonio, TX.

"Your article 'Practicing Acceptance on a Family Trip' was spot on. It really helped me to see how to handle difficult family relationships and suggested very useful tools and phrases. This was the article or email that stood out for me the most. How to get along and still not agree with someone is a very delicate situation. You simplified it quite nicely!" Nancy Schwartz

"I found Michelle to be very helpful and I enjoyed working with her. I was able to talk about all the things I've gone through and see how they were affecting my marriage. I learned that I can't change my husband but I can change myself, my outlook, and how I choose to cope with things. I also learned that I have the perfect right to make myself happy as well!" A. F., San Antonio

"I am a single father of one young son. I made many mistakes in my marriage and my previous relationships but never really knew what I could do to make it better without giving up who I am and what I represent. Michelle has opened my eyes to new perspectives about what I could do better. I had the privilege to read Michelle's new book and I was amazed how thoughtfully, sensitively, and yet right to the point she addresses those issues that make most marriages fail within the first years once the daily routine emerges. Her book is a great compendium for those who are already married and for those who are soon to be married. Michelle's book is one of the best if not THE best source of how to have a happy marriage."
Tom Lehner, Adrian, TX

"You definitely helped to re-frame my ideas about dating. I haven't found 'the one' yet but at least I've made some progress in my attitude about dating and life!" Heather Washburn, Los Angeles, California

"Michelle helped me to do a lot of introspective work and also to see it from the other person's perspective. She was great at repeating what she heard me say to make sure she was following and understood what I was saying. She gave me some excellent book references, which I keep on my nightstand. I enjoyed my sessions with Michelle and have already referred other people to her." Suzie R.

"Working with Michelle gave me hope for my marriage. I realize that it's a lifelong journey and that things may not be solved in one day. I learned how to handle difficult situations and find solutions that worked for me. I have many more good days in my marriage now, and I realize that when we have setbacks, it's not the end. I also learned that it's not selfish to take care of myself and focus on my own happiness." E. D.

"I was nervous at first sharing, but Michelle was kind and understanding. She challenged me to look at my own life and see how my choices affect my relationships and my life. Michelle was most effective in helping me see that "I am important." I realized for the first time in my life that it is ok for me to take time for myself. I was able to work through some very tough and sensitive issues with her without ever feeling vulnerable or afraid. She is really fantastic. Michelle is practiced, insightful and empathetic. She knows her tools and she is wonderful one on one. And she is FUN. Trust this process, and if you are truly willing to be honest, and do the work on yourself, your life will never be the same." Pen G., San Antonio, TX

"Michelle was a blessing to our marriage! Even though we had known each other for years, we had a very difficult time adjusting to living together our first year. Michelle helped us identify the root of our problems and how to better approach our differences. It hasn't always been easy, but thanks to her insights, we have been able to communicate better and more effectively." I.A., San Antonio, TX

Comments from people who attended the Singles Workshops:

"You could use this info in any relationship not just romance. The hand out listing examples of controlling behaviors was good. Interesting to see how subtle it can start out." Deb

"Michelle is a professional in every sense of the word. She is friendly and empathetic to the people in her group and always makes herself available for questions or just a conversation. She does not judge or criticize but rather offers suggestions and encouragement for the well being of the person. The meetings and workshop helped me tremendously. It is not just a focus about finding a mate but discovering who you are in the process and knowing what you want. It's about being a Successful Single in order to be a Successful Couple. In my opinion, Michelle is the best person to get us there!" Ro

"This was fun and informative. It's nice to talk with other people who are single and see how they approach dating. Michelle is very friendly and had good information and material for us. I enjoyed it. Michelle leads an interesting discussion and it is good to hear the experiences of others." Heather

"I felt that it was very informative. I found it helpful to learn about others' experience with dating and learned some valuable information. There were many points shared by other members that I could identify with and agree with." Faisal

Professional friends and their thoughts:

"Michelle is a great coach! She is so easy to talk to, and her warm caring style makes it easy to feel very comfortable talking with her. I highly recommend that you call her for coaching, or sign up for one of her great classes!"

>Leslie Cardinal, Business Coach for Women
>http://LeslieCardinal.com

"Michelle is empathic in all of her work. She's an excellent group facilitator. Because of this, I can imagine how effective she would be one on one."

>Susan K. Morrow, Intuitive Life Teacher and author of
>*Channel One: 137 Messages from the Universe*
>http://www.SusanKMorrow.com

"Michelle understands the dynamics of meeting, dating, falling in love, and marrying someone; she keeps it real. It's not just theory or speculation. Michelle walks her talk."

>Adalia John, Confidence Coach
>Confidence is an Inside Job
>http://www.adaliaconfidenceandsuccessblog.com/

"Michelle's book is unlike any other book available to help couples strengthen their relationships. You can essentially open the book to any page and discover vital information for building a better partnership with your spouse. Yes, you can sit down and read it through from front to back, but given how busy most couples are these days, that's not always possible. You and your partner can set aside a short span of time every day to open the book, pick one of the 81 tips, and work on that together. Do the action steps, practice the affirmations together and watch your relationship grow. It can become your "daily devotional" for happily ever after. I highly recommend Michelle's book!"

>Brenda Zeller, Life and Relationship Coach, EFT Practitioner and Reiki Master
>http://www.vitallifecoaching.com

"Michelle Vasquez does an amazing job at getting at the heart of what could cause a relationship to shift out of the honeymoon stage and draws you into what you can do if you find yourself drifting away from feeling the love between you and your spouse. The love is always there and it truly is a matter of being aware of this and letting the changes bring you to new ways of discovering the love you share together. A recommended read for anyone who wants to make the honeymoon stage last throughout all the years of marriage."

>Gabriella Hartwell, Intuitive Relationship Life Coach and Author of *You Find Your Soul Mate When You Let Go of Searching*.
>www.EmergingSoul.com
>coaching@emergingsoul.com

"Excellent book on relationships! Also an excellent workbook and reference handbook not only for partners but also for anybody's daily personal use to help improve his/her relationships with friends, relatives, colleagues, and most especially, ourselves. Michelle's healing approach and techniques are self-empowering, the exercises are self-revealing that lead to one's better understanding of the dynamics of a relationship. Great tool!"

    Shirley S. Funnamark, RN, MSN, CHTP
    ShFun@aol.com, Anaheim, California

"I've met Michelle on Facebook and first, I was impressed by her gentleness. Every day I was reading her posts and learning something new about emotions, relationships and how we can make it work. Last summer (2010), I invited Michelle as a guest on my radio show and we've discussed relationships from A to Z. She was amazing! Her book is so much better than just one hour on a radio show! She managed to create a wonderful guide that you can use anytime to shape your relationships. It doesn't matter if you are young or old, married, divorced or you're just starting your love life. In any situation you might be, you'll find all the help you need in Michelle's book!"

    Iuliana Lixandru - Medical Intuitive, CNHP
    www.designingabetterlife.com
    iuliana@designingabetterlife.com

"Michelle Vasquez is the perfect relationship coach to teach you how to create - and maintain - the relationship of your dreams. With compassion, insight and clarity, she gives you the necessary tools to guide you out of despair, depression and uncertainty, to hope, fulfillment and love, so that you can build a solid marriage that will last "happily ever after." Dreams really do come true, and Michelle's book is the perfect guide for building a lasting relationship - one that you will want to refer to again and again. It's a gem!"

    Kim Baldwin
    Bodyworker, Holistic Health Practitioner and Wellness Coach
    and co-author of the number one best selling book,
    The Gratitude Book Project: 365 Days of Gratitude
    www.mygenewize.com/kimbaldwin

"Michelle is a respected colleague. I found very early that Michelle believes in the principles of Reality Therapy. What I realized over time, is how committed to these principles she is, and how much she embodies it in her work and her own life. Looking over Michelle's book, it is clear to me that she is writing from her heart, sharing principles she truly believes in, and that she has found helpful in her work. Throughout her book, she encourages readers to take responsibility for their own happiness, and to look more at what they themselves can change, than on what they wish their partner would change. I find her book to be a delightful combination of tips, anecdotes, and personal wisdom for keeping a new couple on track, and helping them know when to seek professional help."

    Kate Boswell, M.S., MFT
    Licensed Marriage and Family Therapist
    kateboswellmft@aol.com
    http://2bstressfree.com

"I've known Michelle Vasquez professionally since 1992 and I know her to be enthusiastic and dedicated. She's a highly skilled professional with great listening skills, as well as the ability to make a difficult concept simple. Michelle will challenge you to improve and assist you in doing so."

    Donna J. Martin, LPC, Certified Clinical Hypnotherapist
    www.donnajmartin.com

Dedication

I dedicate this book to my late husband, Adalberto Vásquez. Without his encouragement I would not have decided to become an entrepreneur and go into private practice as a therapist. He often told me that I needed to write a book. I'm finally honoring his memory by getting my book done!

Al inspired me and encouraged me to develop my speaking and leadership skills. He was the president of Adelante! Toastmaster club in 1998, the year we married. He convinced me to join, and then convinced me to take on a variety of leadership roles. For my first leadership role as the Vice President of Education of our club, he told me I would learn my responsibilities quicker and more thoroughly if I was the one leading the training for that very role. He was right; I had to learn it all very quickly to teach it to others!

Al was like that. He was writing a book for years, but sadly, he died before he was able to have it published. I cannot finish his book, but I honor him by dedicating my book to him. Without Al's love, encouragement, and inspiration, I would not be where I am today, with a completed book. Together we created our very own happily ever after.

I will always love you, my handsome prince!

Acknowledgements

As I've written this book I have been blessed to be reminded that people are willing and even eager to help if I ask. I've also been reminded that writing a book is a project involving many people; it's not just about me. Just as no one is a "self-made" millionaire, no one writes a book all alone. To borrow from a cliché, it takes a village to write a book!

I want to thank the people in my village for their gift of support and encouragement.

I want to thank Marsh Engle, whose coaching for being a contributing author in her most recent book, *Amazing Woman, What's Your Story*, gave me the courage and determination to finally get this book done.

I don't believe I would have actually written my book if not for Donna Kozik's "Write a Book in a Weekend" virtual event. I wrote approximately a fourth of the book during that intensive training. Donna provided the coaching and encouragement, and helped me to believe in myself so I could make my dream a reality. Less than 10 weeks later, I'm done!

Thank you to my "village advisory board" who looked at the manuscript and cover for the book, offering advice, opinions, and an extra set of eyes: Kimberly Enis Webb, Kim Baldwin, Nita Bauer, John Villasana, Leslie Cardinal, Kate Boswell, Frankie Williams, Leta Schmid, Sarah Vásquez, Matthew Enis, Karleene Talley, Tom Lehner, Bobbi Blum Palmer, Brenda Zeller, Iuliana Lixandru, Lisa Kelly-Wilson, Shirley Sangalang Funnamark, Ahna Cleveland, Jerry Woodbridge, and Gabriella Hartwell. A warm thank you, also, to Jim Temple, who responded instantly to my last minute emergency with the cover design and was so gracious in helping me meet my deadline. If I left anyone out, it was not intentional; know that you have my gratitude and appreciation.

I must also thank my parents, Michael and Carolyn Enis. Without their regular trips to Ireland my Dad would not have taken the photo of Kylemore Abbey, my "Happily Ever After Castle," and I would not have had the inspiration to use the photo for the book. Mom said, "I really like that cover because I like the photographer and I like Ireland. Ireland is where Daddy and I have been free to relax and laugh and work on our marriage through the years." My parents have been married for almost 48 years, so they must be doing something right!

CONTENTS

Who is Michelle E. Vásquez?   21
How to get the most out of this book   23

Getting Started:
A Great Marriage Begins With You

Who are the Successful Couples?   29

1. Too many people wait years to get help for a failing marriage.   30
2. Determination alone will not save a failing marriage.   30
3. Filter everything you learn through your own brain before you accept it as "the truth."   31
4. Expect ups and downs as you and your spouse learn new ways to love each other.   31
5. Practice seeing the one you love with loving eyes.   32
6. Marriage isn't easy, but it doesn't have to be like breaking rocks in the hot sun.   33
7. When you are committed to your relationship, you can weather many storms and come out stronger.   35

Section One:
A Happily Ever After Marriage
Doesn't Just Happen; You Create it

8. Great relationships begin with you.   39
9. Lasting change takes time and dedication.   40
10. If your cup is full of your own opinions and beliefs, be willing to empty the cup to learn something new.   42
11. Even the happiest couples have their differences and conflicts.   45
12. It doesn't matter where the problem came from if changing a small behavior gets rid of it.   46
13. If love is all you need then you need a bigger understanding of the word "love."   48

Section Two:
Stumbling Blocks on the Road to Happily Ever After

Bad Childhood?
Your Past Does Not Have to Define Your Present

14	If you had a bad childhood you risk repeating destructive behaviors in your marriage unless you learn how to choose a different path.	55
15	Beware of the Ghosts of Relationships Past who haunt your present interactions with your spouse.	58
16	The skills you learned as a child to protect yourself may not work and may actually be harmful to in your adult relationships.	60

Warning: Are You Slipping Into the Danger Zone?

17	Silent treatment is a violation of your boundaries.	65
18	Be careful about assuming that you know what your spouse is thinking and why your spouse acts a certain way.	69
19	Anger is only an emotion. However, anger becomes a toxic state if you linger there.	70
20	Constructive criticism is an oxymoron.	71
21	Comparing your spouse to others is as fun for her/him as it was when you were compared unfavorably to your siblings growing up.	72

Power Struggles: Do You Want to Be Right or in Harmony?

22	Power struggles keep you on the Hamster Wheel of Conflict.	77
23	Marriage counseling isn't about fixing your spouse.	79
24	Score-keeping is great when you are in competitive sports. It's counterproductive in your marriage.	80
25	Unrealistic expectations can wreak havoc in your relationship.	82

26	"Should" is a four letter word.	84
27	Marriages should be 50/50, right?	86
28	Anger is a "get my way" behavior.	88
29	I have a right to let my anger out or I'll get an ulcer. Is this true?	90
30	When you become stuck in the "fix it" role, it creates an imbalance in your relationship, leading to resentment by both parties.	92
31	There are so many "right" ways to do things; don't quibble over doing it "your" way.	94

Your Beliefs: What Do You Believe In?

32	Your thoughts create your feelings.	99
33	Your opinion is a belief, and may not even be yours to begin with.	101
34	If you are willing to reexamine your beliefs that you're sure are "facts" you can open up some new doors in your relationships.	102
35	Sometimes people believe that a saying is true just because they've heard it so many times.	104

The Story You're Telling Yourself About Your Situation Creates Your Happiness...or Misery

36	The story you're telling yourself about your situation may be keeping you stuck in bitterness and resentment.	109
37	If you're pessimistic about your marriage, be careful about creating a self-fulfilling prophesy.	111
38	How you choose to interpret someone's behavior affects how you feel about that person.	112
39	What you focus on increases. Are you focusing on positive or negative things?	114

Section Three:
Getting Back on the Road to Happily Ever After

Personal Responsibility: If It's To Be It's Up to Me

40 What small thing are you willing to do on a regular and consistent basis, regardless of what your spouse does or doesn't do, that you think will help your relationship? 121
41 If you spend a lot of your time complaining about your spouse to others, you're caught in the Complaint Trap! 123
42 Too many people would rather blame their ex than to look at the other person responsible for the demise of their relationship. 125
43 If it really takes one to tango, you can do wonders for your marriage. 127
44 When you let go of the need to "fix" your spouse, you can concentrate on your personal growth. 129
45 If you believe you are responsible for co-creating a successful marriage, do all you can to make it happen. 131
46 Successful couples take personal responsibility for their thoughts and interpretations. 132
47 If you do not take care of yourself first, you will be in poor shape to take care of anyone else. 134
48 Drop your anger shield and allow love to enter your life. 135
49 Decide what is so important that you absolutely have to keep it. The rest is negotiable. 137
50 Conflict, while uncomfortable, can teach you so much about yourself. 140

Self-Control: When "That's Just the Way I Am" Won't Cut it Anymore

51 Exercising self-control is a cornerstone of a happy, successful relationship. 145
52 Self-improvement is a wonderful endeavor. "Fixing" others is not. 148
53 Even though you're married you still need to mind your manners. 149

54	"Judge not that ye be not judged" is a good rule for marriage.	152
55	I feel bad so I get to treat you badly? In which universe, exactly, is this okay?	154
56	When you are committed to your own self-growth, it gets easier to let go of the need to fix others.	156
57	Words can soothe or they can be terrible weapons.	158
58	Just as in carpentry "measure twice, cut once" works well when speaking. Measure your words twice before you speak.	159
59	A closed mouth gathers no foot.	160
60	Just because you think it doesn't mean you must speak it.	161
61	Do you believe in total honesty? What if what you want to say is not helpful? Or just an opinion?	162
62	Most stuff is small stuff. Don't make mountains out of molehills.	163
63	Express your point of view and then let go of the need to have your spouse do what you think s/he should do.	165
64	If you make a decision that you think is sound, let go of the need for your spouse to agree with you.	167

Compassion: Walk a Mile in Your Spouse's Shoes

65	Take a walk in your spouse's shoes for a day and see what you learn.	173
66	Do unto others as they need to be done unto.	174
67	You and your spouse have two different brains, so you're going to see things differently.	175
68	Men and women speak different languages. Learning the language of your spouse creates a strong connection.	176
69	Sometimes panic looks like anger. Strive to remain calm when your partner looks angry but is possibly scared.	178

Passion: Keep the Fire Burning Brightly

70	Daily appreciation of the little things your spouse does goes a long way to create goodwill in your marriage.	181
71	Handle your marriage the way you would handle a newborn baby, carefully. It is a treasure.	182

72	It's hard to be sexually intimate with the one you love when you are holding onto bitterness and resentment.	183
73	Reignite the passion in your marriage by asking for what you want and expressing appreciation for what you like.	185
74	Date night is especially important if you have small children.	188
75	Keeping a familiar routine for your children allows you and your spouse to have Grown Up Time together in the evening.	189

Conflict Resolution: Creating Harmony at Home

76	How badly do you want to win the argument? Enough to lose the relationship?	193
77	When you hurt the one you love, be quick to apologize.	194
78	Reflective listening is a gift you give to each other to understand on a deeper level.	196
79	Avoid looking at the one you love with the "the look that kills."	200
80	Boxers take a break every three minutes. Why not give your marriage a break when you are in conflict?	204

Creating Your Very Own Happily Ever After

| 81 | Write your own love story with generous helpings of appreciation, admiration, and gratitude. | 209 |

Recommended Reading   213

Who is Michelle Vásquez?

Michelle Vásquez is a Licensed Professional Counselor and Relationship Coach with over 21 years experience working with both couples and singles. She has helped hundreds of people improve their relationships by asking them the hard questions that guide them to solve their problems in new and creative ways. Her passion is helping you create love that lasts a lifetime.

She works with couples who want to make sure their honeymoon lasts beyond that trip to the Bahamas after they said "I Do." She also works with couples who have been married for decades who are eager to bring back joy and fun into their marriage.

She is committed to helping singles who may be divorced or may have never married. They may have had a series of failed relationships and wonder why they cannot make it work. They may be widowed and want to find love again after loss, whether it be romantic, platonic, or simply the rediscovery of self-love during their grief journey after loss.

Her True Love Relationship Coaching Program for Singles who want to find the love of their life begins by teaching them to do some deep self-reflection to understand and begin to remove the obstacles they have unknowingly put in their path. The next step is to create a workable dating plan to find, attract, and keep their ideal partner. Once they have found someone to date, the work transitions into helping them to determine if the person is right for them and teaching them relationship building tools.

True Love Relationship Program: Creating Happily Ever After is for couples who want to keep the passion alive in their marriage. Because you always bring yourself into any relationship you have, your work with Michelle begins with you working on your relationship with yourself.

Michelle's True Love Relationship Coaching programs, workshops, and products were created for people who are serious about finding, attracting, and keeping love in their lives. The work is an "action learning course." Her clients are encouraged to take serious and consistent action.

No excuses anymore, just a very different way of thinking and full support while you achieve this incredibly exciting goal: getting a crystal clear vision of your life and your purpose, truly knowing and understanding yourself in new and exciting ways, and opening yourself to receiving love into your life so that you can create a happy, successful relationship with the one for you.

Michelle received her Master of Science in Counseling Psychology from Our Lady of the Lake University, San Antonio, Texas, in 1993. She has worked as a Licensed Professional Counselor in Texas since 1997. In 2001 she left the Family Violence Prevention Services, where she worked for eight years, to begin her private practice working with couples and singles. She received her coaching training with the Relationship Coaching Institute.

Michelle focuses mainly on the present, using Solution Oriented modalities to help her clients solve their immediate challenges. She teaches her clients Choice Theory, created by William Glasser, MD. She believes that everyone has the ability to solve his/her own problems. Her job is to ask the powerful questions that allow her clients to think in new and creative ways, thus coming up with their own solutions to the challenges that they face.

Michelle resides in San Antonio, Texas, where she has a private practice. She has two cats and loves to dance ballroom and Salsa.

How to Get the Most Out of This Book

You may have been attracted to this book because you want to make sure that you have many tools to help you create a wonderfully successful marriage. If so, I commend you.

Far too many people wait until things are very wrong in their relationships and have been wrong for sometimes years or even decades. Only then do they seek to make things better and often their solution is to call a divorce lawyer.

If you are reading this book, chances are that you are looking for answers. You want to help your marriage and you want to improve your connection with your spouse. You remember what it was like when you first met and you want those loving feelings back.

I congratulate you! I am so glad you are on this journey of self-improvement. Your marriage improves when you work on what you can do to help it.

If you have done any of the following things, you can appreciate how much time, effort, energy, and (most likely) money goes into seeing these things through to the finish:

- ☐ Receiving a college degree
- ☐ Finishing trade school
- ☐ Graduating from high school or receiving your GED
- ☐ Becoming an entrepreneur
- ☐ Training for a marathon/running in a marathon
- ☐ Competing in sports
- ☐ Learning a new language
- ☐ Quitting smoking
- ☐ Successfully following a weight reduction program
- ☐ Learning ballroom dancing
- ☐ Raising children

Essentially, if you have learned any new skill, you recognize that it takes some effort and commitment to the task if you want to own that skill. The same is true for relationships. If you want to improve your communication and conflict resolution skills with the one you love, you know you have to commit to learning and applying these new skills.

If you have done anything in your life worth doing, you realize you had to stick to it. Remember, you didn't get it right the first time, the second or 10th time, or maybe even the 50th time. When you feel discouraged, think about this quote by Thomas Edison, "I have not failed. I've just found 10,000 ways that won't work." He was a man who knew the importance of persistence when doing something of value.

That's all right. How many years do Olympic competitors practice before they enter the games? How long do you think it took Michael Jordan to become the basketball player he is today? And get this: even those gold medalists and those state champions still have coaches. They still continue to train so that they can get better and better.

In your work you have on the job training and maybe annual requirements for continuing education, right?

Do you see where I'm going with this? Just because you said "I do" doesn't mean it's all hearts and flowers from now on. Now you get down to the business of living your life as a couple and that requires some continuing education.

Believe it or not, this is good news!

Why would this be good news? Because like everything else worth keeping, focusing on your relationship allows you to continue to do what you do to create and keep the relationship going strong.

Your car won't continue to run as perfectly as it did when it was brand new and you drove it off the lot. You wouldn't expect it to. You know you have to maintain your car to keep it running well with regular oil changes, tire rotations, and other regularly scheduled repairs.

Give your marriage the same attention you would give to learning a new hobby or sport and maintain it the way you would your car. If you do these things, your relationship will be one of joy. It doesn't mean you will never have setbacks. It means that you will be better prepared to deal with the inevitable bumps life will occasionally throw under your feet.

Use this book as a guide. Keep a regular journal of your progress. You will find action steps throughout this book. Some of them are things you can work on alone. If you aren't doing it already, I encourage you to get a journal and write out your responses to the questions in this book in your journal.

Some of the action steps are for couples and are problem-solving tools. Use the ones that fit best with your needs and style. It's quite all right if you experiment and modify things to work best for you.

This book is a quick read if you just want some quick tips and tools. You can also use it as a workbook. The action steps help you to think and to start creating your very own happily ever after in your relationship.

I encourage you to use your journal to record your thoughts, feelings, reflections, insights, and even epiphanies you may have as you read this book and answer the questions. Most of the questions I pose are thought-provoking. I help my clients by guiding them to find their own answers. I do this by asking them questions that make them think.

These questions are not easy to answer at times. That's the beauty of the questions; if they were easy, you would not learn much from your answers. These questions challenge you to question what you believe to be "true" and to find new ways to think. When you think in new ways you begin to change what you do.

One more thing: remember to stay in the Adult Role as you learn these new exercises and techniques. Eric Berne, MD, father of Transactional Analysis, explained that when people interact, they do so in three different ways. They act as a Parent, as an Adult, or as a Child.

These three words are capitalized because they are roles, or ego states, not actual parents, children, or adults. As two adults in your marriage, it is important that you recognize which state you are in when you interact. Are you in the Parent role or the Child role? Your ideal state when interacting with each other is Adult to Adult.

When you are in your Parent state, you act, think, and feel as if you were the parent, possibly scolding or wagging your finger at your spouse. You may be responding to your spouse who may be engaging in the Child role. A person in the Child state will act, think, and feel similarly to how they did in childhood. The Adult state is the rational one in which you are able to behave more objectively, logically, and maturely. Your task is to be aware of which role you are playing in your interactions and to learn to remain in the Adult role.

I hope you get exactly what you need from this book. I wish you the best of success in your journey to create a loving, happy relationship with the one you love.

I appreciate you and I wish you joy in your marriage,
Michelle

Getting Started:

A Great Marriage Begins With You

"Success in marriage does not come merely through finding the right mate, but through being the right mate." Barnett R. Brickner

Who are the Successful Couples?

If you want to be part of a successful, happy couple, begin by creating a vision together of your ideal relationship. Here are some thoughts about what successful, happy couples are and what they do to create and maintain their very own happily ever after:

- ☐ Successful couples know that self-growth is a lifelong journey.
- ☐ Successful couples are flexible.
- ☐ Successful couples understand the importance of negotiating differences.
- ☐ Successful couples seek first to understand.
- ☐ Successful couples know that conflict is inevitable, but fighting is optional.
- ☐ Successful couples know that seeking help is a sign of courage and strength.
- ☐ Successful couples know they will hurt each other, though not intentionally.
- ☐ Successful couples understand that blame and criticism destroy relationships.
- ☐ Successful couples know that they are responsible for their own behavior and do not try to control each other.
- ☐ Successful couples make mistakes like everyone else, and they see them as learning experiences.
- ☐ Successful couples understand the value of compassion.
- ☐ Successful couples understand the value of a sincere apology.
- ☐ Successful couples honor their agreements.
- ☐ Successful couples understand the difference between total, blunt honesty and discretion.
- ☐ Successful couples know they can count on each other in difficult times.
- ☐ Successful couples forgive themselves and each other.
- ☐ Successful couples understand the value of inter-dependence.
- ☐ Successful couples don't get it right all the time and they are okay with that.
- ☐ Successful couples know that great relationships begin with the two individuals in the marriage.

> **1. Too many people wait years to seek help for a failing marriage.**

As a therapist, I am always sad when people come to my office as a last ditch effort to save their marriage. Too often, they are just one step away from hiring a divorce attorney, yet they want to say, "We tried everything." They have waited so long to seek help to get their marriage back on track that it's like someone asking for help to fix the foundation of their house after the house is already on fire.

This does not mean that they cannot be helped. It just means that we have to wade through years of anger, bitterness, and resentment to discover the core love that may be still buried underneath. Often they are unwilling to do the work that is necessary, they feel terribly discouraged, and they are ready to give up. Don't let this be your story!

> **2. Determination alone will not save a failing marriage.**

Don't fool yourself into thinking you've already done "everything" to help your marriage. This is what I have found when people tell me "We've done everything and nothing works." What is usually closer to the truth is that they have done a few things repeatedly and become frustrated with their inability to resolve their differences. When the few things they know to do have failed to get the results they want, they have done them again and again. Harder, louder, and faster.

No wonder they are frustrated! I don't blame them. They don't know what else to do and they are afraid all is lost. Most of the time these are creative people. They are able to do some serious problem-solving at work or with their children. They just need to be reminded of just how creative they are.

So we work together to come up with solutions. These solutions are tailor-made for them. It's amazing how often they are able to come up with their own new and creative ways to help their marriage once they are able to unlock their own abilities and resources.

> **3. Filter everything you learn through your own brain before you accept it as "the truth."**

It's important when you read or learn something new that you avoid jumping on the bandwagon without examining each new piece of information. Check it out and make sure it fits with your values. This includes what you read in this book. I do not expect you to accept everything I say without questioning it.

I often tell my clients that they need to decide what works for them. My job is to be a guide. I ask my clients thought-provoking questions to help them get their own creative juices flowing. This allows them to find their own solutions.

I cannot live your life for you, nor would you want me to. What I suggest may not work for you. That's all right. Find your own truth. You have to take what you learn and figure out what you want to keep and what you want to let go of (or set aside to think about later).

It's great to be excited about something new you have learned. Keep in mind that your spouse may not share your enthusiasm. That's all right, too. Just as you have a right to learn and grow at your own pace, so does your spouse. You have a right to have a different point of view and so does your spouse.

> **4. Expect ups and downs as you and your spouse learn new ways to love each other.**

The path to creating a loving relationship is not a straight and easy one. Be gentle with yourself as you learn and grow.

When my clients and I create a plan together that they are going to work on in between our meetings, I caution them that they may experience setbacks as they try out new behaviors and work the plan for improving their connection with each other. So when they stumble, they (hopefully) feel less discouraged and sometimes even say, "Oh, yeah, Michelle told us to expect this."

Learning new communication skills takes time and regular effort. You and your spouse can help each other by forgiving yourselves and each other as you stumble and learn. If you are expecting perfection of yourself, let that go. Laugh when you practice your new skills. Keep going. It's going to feel awkward, as if you were the worst actors in a bad play! However, what feels awkward now will get easier as you continue to practice. Soon, you will own your new relationship skills.

I want to be your cheerleader. I am excited about your journey and I want you to enjoy it. You will do some hard work and eventually what you are learning will become part of who you are. Remember, at one point in your young life you didn't know how to read, but you learned. Now you read without even thinking about it. At one point you knew nothing about being a parent, cooking, or doing the work you do, but you learned.

Life is like that. There's always room to learn more. So be proud of yourself and keep learning! Hooray for you!

5. Practice seeing the one you love with loving eyes.

A loving relationship can go a long way to heal the hurts of the past.
When you are in a loving relationship:

- ☐ You trust each other enough to be vulnerable instead of defensive.
- ☐ You are able to explore past hurts and let them go.
- ☐ You can grow together as you co-create the relationship of your dreams.

When you are able to trust the one you're with:

- ☐ You can allow yourself to let down your guard.
- ☐ You understand that your spouse is not going to repeat the hurts of the past, at least not intentionally.
- ☐ You can begin to redefine yourself with your partner and let go of previous pain.
- ☐ It may be scary to be this vulnerable, but it gets easier as you go along and build positive experiences together.

With the help of someone you have chosen to trust, you can explore past hurts. Letting go of the pain of the past is never a straight path. Inside your loving relationship, you can choose new patterns to replace the old ones that did not work for you. When you both turn toward each other with support and acceptance, you don't have to reach for defensiveness as your first reaction.

You and your spouse have an amazing opportunity to grow as a couple. You get to work together to create a happy, passionate relationship. The rewards of this growth work are limitless and you are able to do this because you trust the one you love. You get to decide to break the negative patterns of your respective pasts and live in a way that suits the two of you best.

It's not easy to do this and often, even if couples have the best of intentions, they need outside help to create this wonderful, trusting life together. That's where relationship coaching comes in handy. You can create your vision for your relationship and set your goals for living the life you've dreamed of with the one you love.

6. Marriage isn't easy, but it doesn't have to be like breaking rocks in the hot sun.

Too many people struggle needlessly when there is so much help available to them. They are blocked by unhelpful beliefs such as:

- ☐ It's nobody's business.
- ☐ We can handle it ourselves.
- ☐ Don't air your dirty laundry in public.
- ☐ It's a sign of weakness to ask for help.
- ☐ I should know what to do in my marriage.

The problem with this is your "marriage manual" was handed to you by parents and grandparents who often had no clue how to create a happy marriage. Maybe they endured a painful marriage or maybe they gave up and divorced when you were young. And that was your training for creating a marriage!

This unwritten marriage manual created your beliefs about marriage, many of which are entirely unhelpful. Therefore, it's up to you to write your own marriage manual with new knowledge.

Action step:

- ☐ To get started, examine the lessons you learned from the adults who taught you about marriage, directly or indirectly.
- ☐ How did your parents interact with each other? Your answer will give you insight into what you expect (or fear) from your own marriage.
- ☐ Which patterns are you repeating?
- ☐ Which patterns are you aware of that you are deliberately striving to change?

Congratulate yourself for your insights. You are beginning to consciously create something new!

Affirmation: As I learn new skills, my marriage becomes more joyful and fun!

7. When you are committed to your relationship, you can weather many storms and come out stronger.

Are you committed to your relationship "for better or worse"? Or do you give up too easily? Recently I watched a video on You Tube of a research team that set up a very complicated obstacle course for squirrels who were trying to get to some birdseed. You would think that the squirrels would give up and go foraging for nuts, but these squirrels hung in there and kept trying until they figured out how to get to the food.

The squirrels were singularly focused on their target. They didn't stop to think; they just kept persisting when they saw a sure source of food rather than go off and seek other food sources that may or may not yield results. They just did what squirrels do, sticking to their task and working toward their goal of getting at the food they could see. Their persistence paid off, although it took over a day of trying.

After seeing the squirrels go through the obstacle course, I wonder what drives us humans, especially in relationships. Too many people give up too easily. Marriages have become disposable. Too many people are thinking, "It's too hard; I'll just divorce and find someone better." Divorcing with the thought that someone better will come along is a fantasy. The elusive search for the greener grass often proves to be painfully long, fruitless, and ultimately lonely.

What is your marriage worth to you? Are you as persistent as this squirrel? In the book, *The Case for Marriage: Why Married People are Happier, Healthier, and Better Off Financially* by Linda J. Waite and Maggie Gallagher, the authors researched why marriages last.

As they interviewed couples, they discovered that the ones who simply persisted, holding the marriage together despite hardships, disagreements, and unhappiness, were happier when they interviewed those same couples again five years later. In other words, they were committed to making their marriage work.

These couples didn't go to marriage counseling. They didn't necessarily do anything different. They just decided that their marriage was important enough to weather the "worst" parts of "for better or worse." They didn't have a back up plan. They didn't declare they would get a divorce if things didn't work out.

No, these couples believed they had made a commitment to their marriage and so they kept at it. Eventually they found that the rough times began to get easier. They withstood the storm. Most likely, they were stronger for it.

Sheer stubbornness to keep their marriage together had made a difference! Do you give up too easily or are you like the squirrel? Are you going to give your marriage your all? I hope so.

Action step:

- ☐ If you have been pessimistic about your marriage, change your mind. Be like that squirrel.
- ☐ Remember that marriage, like life, has normal ups and downs. It's all right.

Affirmation: I am committed to my marriage like the squirrel is committed to getting to the food. I persist.

Section One:

A Happily Ever After Marriage Doesn't Just Happen. You Create it.

"Be patient with yourself. Self-growth is tender; it's holy ground. There is no greater investment." Stephen Covey

8. Great relationships begin with you.

You've heard it takes two to tango and maybe you have even read some self-improvement books that tell you it only takes one to tango. My opinion is that the truth lies somewhere in the middle. However, I do believe that if you are the only one in your relationship who is interested in making it better, you can do a lot to create a happy relationship.

The wonderful thing about you learning new skills, tools, and techniques to bring into your relationship is that when you change what you do, you are bound to affect others. If you have learned to stop and think instead of automatically shouting or pouting, your partner is going to act differently in response to your change of behavior.

Action step:

- ☐ Start with a simple willingness to improve yourself.
- ☐ Learn all you can that will help you improve your behavior.
- ☐ Go slow and be kind to yourself as you learn.
- ☐ Ask for help when you need it, either by finding a therapist, a relationship coach, reading a self-improvement book, attending a workshop, etc.

Affirmation: I am the change I want to see in my relationship.

9. Lasting change takes time and dedication.

Just as you cannot prepare for a marathon in a weekend, you cannot expect that the new skills you are learning will instantly become part of how you respond during conflict in your marriage. Improvements take time. You cannot lose 20 pounds overnight. You cannot learn a new language in a day. You don't have the ability to program your brain for instantaneous success.

Again, I encourage you to be gentle with yourself and your spouse while you are making the changes that will make your marriage great. Forgive yourselves as you try out new behaviors because you will not get them right instantly.

While I'm not saying that it takes years for you to rebuild trust and intimacy in your marriage, I am asking you to keep your expectations realistic. If you have spent years engaging in tearing down your relationship, you cannot expect it will get fixed in one session with a therapist. I tell my clients that I cannot wave my magic wand and instantly make it all better. Nor can they take a pill to dissolve conflicts.

You will probably leave a weekend retreat with a lot of great feelings toward each other, but unless you are committed to using the new tools you have gained there on a regular basis, you will find that you quickly slip back into your default behaviors.

I blame the fast food industry for creating within many people the expectation of instant gratification: "I want it now and I want it hot and tasty." In the movie "The Matrix," Neo, the protagonist, had a port in the back of his head that allowed him (and others like him) to plug into computer programs. The people in this story could download any knowledge they wanted into their brains. In one scene, Neo's brain was downloaded with fighting skills. In a matter of seconds he knew everything about a variety of martial arts and all types of combat training. Not only did he have perfect knowledge, he had instant muscle memory to execute his new skills.

Wouldn't it be fantastic if you could get an instant download of how to behave in such a way that will insure that you create a happy, successful marriage? Of course! But, unlike Neo, you don't have a plug in the back of your head to download that kind of information. So you're stuck with learning new skills and practicing them. Even worse, you must practice your new skills at a slow and uneven pace. You are not going to get them right the first time. That's all right. Keep working on it. This is not a bad thing. What you learn thoroughly, you own!

When I work with my clients I ask them to come up with some small steps (just one at a time) that they can do to move closer to feeling better toward each other. Just as you cannot ask a child who doesn't know his ABC's to read a novel, you cannot ask a couple who is stuck in bad feelings about each other to "just feel good toward each other."

I work with my clients to help them discover how to recover those good feelings they once had for each other. So we have to begin by addressing the interactions and behaviors that are preventing them from feeling good about each other.

If you are actively trying to control and fix each other you are unlikely to feel warm and fuzzy toward each other. You are more likely to be stuck in resentment, anger, and blame.

Action step:

- ☐ Work on one new behavior at a time.
- ☐ Take small steps to insure your progress.
- ☐ Let go of expecting perfection.
- ☐ Celebrate your progress with lots of praise and appreciation.

Affirmation: I am gentle with myself and my spouse as we learn new behaviors that help our relationship.

10. If your cup is full of your own opinions and beliefs, be willing to empty the cup to learn something new.

Maybe you've heard the story of the professor who visits an elderly Zen Buddhist and has tea with him. The professor wants to talk with the Zen Buddhist about his wisdom. The elderly teacher pours tea into the professor's cup until it begins to overflow and then he continues to pour. The professor, who has been watching anxiously, finally cries out, "The cup is full. It's overflowing. No more will go in."

The Zen master responds, "Like this cup, you are full of your own ideas, opinions, and beliefs. How can I teach you unless you first empty your cup?"

The wise man tells the seeker his cup is already full and that if he is to learn he needs to empty his cup of what he thinks he knows. Similarly, my task is to help those whose minds are filled with unhelpful and, at times, harmful beliefs. I teach them tools to get unstuck so they can stop repeating the same unhelpful patterns.

Who are the people who have the most success in therapy or relationship coaching? These are people who:

- ☐ Are willing to examine their assumptions critically.
- ☐ Are willing to accept that they can learn something new.
- ☐ Are eager to do something different when necessary.
- ☐ Are open to letting go of the habits that are keeping them stuck and often miserable.

As you entered romantic relationships in your teens or early adulthood, you formed many ideas based on what people told you and what you witnessed. Some of these ideas became beliefs. Beliefs can be helpful or harmful.

People are social creatures and they seek to connect with others. Even if you experienced traumatic beginnings, you still want to connect with an intimate partner. You may think that you can do better than your parents. You may believe that you can have a happy relationship. And that's wonderful. It does start with a belief in yourself that you can have joy in your life and in your relationship.

Here's the thing: you will have much better success creating a happy relationship once you understand how to counter the beliefs that are holding you back and how to create a new way of understanding relationships.

You were given a certain set of tools that may have left you guarded. It's hard to have an intimate relationship when you are keeping your shield up. That shield is a huge barrier to intimacy. I hope that you are aware that if you want something to change, the change begins with you.

Action step:

Use your journal to write your assumptions about relationships. This is something you will need to come back to periodically, since it is unlikely that you will cover all of your assumptions at once. These are beliefs that you began to form early in your life, watching influential adults in your life, beginning with your parents.

What did you learn about relationships early in your life? Were they:

- ☐ Loving?
- ☐ Based on mutual respect?
- ☐ Scary?
- ☐ Filled with drama and heartache?
- ☐ Controlling?

Based on what you saw early in your life, how did this shape how you thought about relationships? Did you learn:

- ☐ That you wanted a marriage just like your parents?
- ☐ That a happy marriage is possible and can last a lifetime?
- ☐ That men/women are honorable, trustworthy, respectful, kind, loving, generous, happy together, faithful, etc?
- ☐ That women/men are dangerous, manipulative, weak, helpless, scary, controlling, drunk, untrustworthy, cheaters, abandoners, etc?
- ☐ That marriage is to be avoided at all costs (or not worth the pain)?
- ☐ That marriage doesn't last?

Examine the answers you have written to these questions. What have you learned about yourself as a result?

Affirmation: I am open to examining the beliefs that are holding me back from creating a happy, successful relationship.

11. Even the happiest couples have their differences and conflicts.

If you believe that you shouldn't argue, you are going to be in for a shock when you do. Living with someone will inevitably create friction. That's normal and it's OK. If you were taught that arguing is bad, you may want to suppress it or ignore it. I'm going to tell you that it's OK to argue. It's what you do with it and how you argue that can create renewed calm or more stormy weather.

John Gottman, PhD, has studied couples for over 20 years in his Love Lab to determine what keeps them together or tears them apart. What fascinates me is that he found that couples who argue loudly and often are not necessarily more likely to divorce than couples who avoid arguing at all costs or couples who rationally and calmly discuss and negotiate their differences.

Dr. Gottman says that when four behaviors he calls the Four Horsemen of the Apocalypse become entrenched habits, the couple is likely to end their relationship if they are unwilling to change these destructive behaviors. These behaviors are contempt, defensiveness, criticism, and stonewalling.

Action step:

- ☐ Learn some healthy conflict resolution skills. Sometimes doing things on your own is enough. Other times you need more help to cement the new behaviors. It's important to have the wisdom to discern when you need a helping hand.
- ☐ Understand that conflict is normal. Arguing is optional.

Affirmation: I accept that conflict is normal. I am willing to learn new skills and apply them to be a part of the solution when conflict arises.

> **12. It doesn't matter where the problem came from if changing a small behavior gets rid of it.**

You don't have to spend years in therapy to solve immediate problems in the here and now. This is a tenet of Solution-Oriented Therapy. Insight is helpful. It's that "aha moment" in which you realize that the origin of your life-long fear of dogs began when you were six years old and a neighbor's golden retriever growled at you when you entered her yard.

However, insight alone doesn't help you make a plan to do something different. If you have the time and resources to spend years in therapy, go for it. There is nothing wrong with that if it's what you want to do. Here's the thing: Insight is only part of the process. Your next step is to create an action plan to insure you keep progressing. The step that follows is doing what you have planned:

Here is a breakdown of the process of creating a change:

- ☐ Think about the problem and gain some insight.
- ☐ Create a workable action plan for making the necessary changes.
- ☐ Follow the plan step by step.

Most people, when faced with a problem, want it resolved yesterday. The hard part about solving a problem is the third part, which is following the plan. I believe you can make some pretty good progress quickly if you are willing to look at the problem in new and creative ways and follow through. Most of my clients who follow through with the plan they have created make significant progress in six to twelve sessions.

Action step:

Think about a particular problem you are dealing with:

- ☐ How are you currently trying to fix this problem? Often your solution to a problem IS the problem. The solution is not working and maintains the problem.
- ☐ Brainstorm other possible ways to solve the problem in your journal and talk to your spouse about what other ways the two of you can come up with to solve the problem.
- ☐ Look for the exceptions. When is the problem not a problem? Or when is it less of a problem? What is happening at this time?
- ☐ Is the way you are thinking about the problem causing (or even maintaining) the problem? Sometimes your beliefs about the problem keep the problem alive.

Affirmation: I focus on solutions. I examine my beliefs around the problems in my life. I know that I can find a solution. I am committed to following through with my plan of action.

13. If love is all you need then you need a bigger understanding of the word "love."

When I hear "love is all you need" I think of romantic love. If you think of love as only an emotion, it will fade. It is important to expand your understanding of love beyond just another feeling. It is an action.

Many years ago I had a young client in my office, a professional man in his early 30's, who was seeking counseling because he wondered if the woman he was with was the right one for him. He has been dating her for about six months. He said, "We fight constantly, but we love each other."

The more he told me about his situation, the clearer the picture got. The sexual chemistry between them was great. I suggested that perhaps he was confusing lust with love. This is quite common. This chemistry is what initially attracts you to someone and it feels great. A word of caution: great chemistry doesn't necessarily mean you will be compatible in a long-term relationship.

If you do not have an understanding of love that is much bigger than the "feeling" you get when you are around that person, you may find a budding relationship quickly dying on the vine the first time you disagree with each other. Lust without a deeper connection plus bad feelings that surface when you argue cannot withstand the test of time.

Unless you develop a deeper sense of connection to your spouse that allows you to continue to love despite not necessarily liking him/her in the moment, you are not going to make it in your marriage.

After years of marriage, my late husband and I would rarely argue. Sometimes I would think to myself, "I love Al, but right now I don't like him very much." My love for him remained strong regardless of whether I was happy with him at that moment. If you find that you are in a love/hate relationship with your spouse, beware. Your understanding of the word "love" may need expansion.

Love is one of humanity's favorite topics. Romantic, filial, and platonic love have been written about in abundance. I like the way love is explained in 1 Corinthians 13.

> Love is patient.
> Love is kind.
> Love does not envy.
> Love does not boast.
> Love is not proud.
> Love does not dishonor others.
> Love is not self-seeking.
> Love is not easily angered.
> Love keeps no record of wrongs.
> Love does not delight in evil
> but rejoices with the truth.
> Love always protects.
> Love always trusts.
> Love always hopes.
> Love always perseveres.
> Love never fails.

This looks like a lot to live up to. I don't expect anyone to love perfectly. No one can. Striving to understand that love means a lot more than how you feel in the moment is a step in the right direction. Also, notice that all of these descriptions of the word "love" are actions, not feelings.

Action step:

- ☐ Examine your personal beliefs around the concept of love. Do your beliefs need to be expanded to include some of the above descriptions of love?
- ☐ Write your insights in your journal.
- ☐ Pick one aspect of love you would like to focus on this week and decide on some action steps to create love in your relationship.

Affirmation: I expand my concept of love. Love is a verb and I can show love through my loving actions.

Section Two:

Stumbling Blocks on the Road to Happily Ever After

"When you are in the final days of your life, what will you want? Will you hug that college degree in the walnut frame? Will you ask to be carried to the garage so you can sit in your car? Will you find comfort in rereading your financial statement? Of course not. What will matter then will be people. If relationships will matter most then, shouldn't they matter most now?" Max Lucado

Bad Childhood?

Your Past Does Not Have to Define Your Present

"Love is the biggest eraser there is. Love erases even the deepest imprinting because love goes deeper than anything. If your childhood imprinting was very strong, and you keep saying, 'It's their fault. I can't change,' you stay stuck." Louise L. Hay

> **14. If you had a bad childhood you risk repeating destructive behaviors in your marriage unless you learn how to choose a different path.**

Xena: "I let my fear and hatred blind me to everything."
Gabrielle: "Sometimes the past can do that. Xena, if I had been through what you've been through…"
Xena: "No. No! You understand hatred, but you've never given into it. You don't know how much I love that."

Excerpt from "The Price," a second season episode of "Xena: Warrior Princess."

I love Xena! I've discovered some pretty profound life lessons in this show, despite the campy, silly nature of many of the episodes.

I have worked with many couples who experienced some pretty difficult childhoods. They were, understandably, having a tough time in their marriage because they had no idea how to create a happy one. If they grew up in an environment of fear and hatred, they tended to re-create the same thing in their adult relationships.

Often my clients who have been brought up in difficult situations lived in fear of the very people who were supposed to nurture and protect them. Like Xena, they were filled with fear and hatred, and they spewed anger at anyone who tried to get close to them. Some learned hatred at their parents' knee.

Many adults came from dysfunctional homes, surviving horrifying childhood experiences such as:

- ☐ Neglect
- ☐ Physical, sexual, and/or emotional and verbal abuse
- ☐ Alcoholic and/or drug addicted parents
- ☐ Parents who raged at each other and at the children
- ☐ Self-absorbed parents who were more concerned with themselves than their children
- ☐ Severely mentally ill parents
- ☐ Reversal of parent-child roles (the child had to take care of the parent and/or siblings) often beginning at a very early age

Growing up in a chaotic situation leaves scars. Many adults who lived through these situations grew up thinking their experience was normal. Some realized that something was wrong, but were powerless to change it. Either way, fear and hatred can become part of their adult life unless they are able to take a good look at their childhood experience and choose whether to remain a victim or to learn and grow from the experience.

Louise L. Hay says, "We are all victims of victims." Your parents may not have known any better than to repeat the pattern of victimization they experienced at the hands of their parents. They did the best they could with the knowledge they had at the time. Even if you wish they had done a better job, learned some new skills, or did anything different, it is what it is and the past cannot be changed.

However, you can decide what you will do right now, in the present. You are reading this book, so I'm thinking you must be interested in learning new skills. You recognize there are plenty of other things you can do besides mindlessly repeating destructive behaviors.

At some point you may be faced with a choice to keep blaming your parents for your rotten childhood or to decide what you are going to do with yourself. Your childhood experiences affect your adult relationships, and if it was a rotten one, you have probably repeated a lot of the destructive patterns.

It is perfectly understandable if you feel righteous anger toward either or both of your parents. At some point you may feel the need to let go of that anger, especially if it is keeping you stuck and unable to progress in your self-growth journey. Holding onto anger about your past is always going to affect your personal relationships, especially your marriage.

The danger of staying stuck in the fear and hatred is that you risk re-creating a similar situation with your spouse. Your spouse is in danger of becoming a stand in for your parent. You may be re-enacting the fear and hatred with your spouse, even if your spouse has not done anything (other than trigger an old response in you).

Be careful to avoid seeing your spouse through the lens of your interactions with your parents or past intimate partners. You may have married someone similar to one or both of your parents, but that person is not the same.

The wonderful thing about a loving marriage is that you can work through a lot of pain from your past in a safe, intimate context. Your spouse cannot save you, nor can your spouse fix you. But you can experience healing and growth in the context of a marriage that you choose to create together.

Action step:

The first step toward making a change is to acknowledge the need for a change. If you now recognize that you are repeating the destructive patterns of your childhood, you have taken that first step.

- ☐ Use your journal to write about your insights. How are you repeating the negative patterns of your childhood?
- ☐ If you have no idea what to do next that's all right. You are on the right track. Give yourself a pat on the back for beginning the journey of recovering and creating a new path for yourself and your adult relationships.
- ☐ Talk with your spouse about your insights about how your childhood upbringing and old behavior patterns and triggers are affecting your marriage.
- ☐ Keep learning. Begin with books about childhood abuse and recovery.
- ☐ Join support groups that deal with childhood abuse and recovery.
- ☐ Hire a therapist to address the things you need extra help with.

Affirmation: I acknowledge that my childhood affects my adult relationships. I agree to be patient with myself as I learn new, helpful ways of relating in my marriage.

15. Beware of the Ghosts of Relationships Past who haunt your present interactions with your spouse.

We all have Ghosts of Relationships Past who interfere with our interactions the ones we love. Your ghosts may be living or dead, but they are always alive in your present relationships. That is, as long as you are living unconsciously. Bringing these ghosts into your conscious awareness is the first step in recognizing how they affect your interactions with those you love.

Your interactions with important people in your early life affect how you see your spouse. You learned a lot about relationships by watching your mother and father. The way your father and mother treated you affects how you treat your spouse and how you interpret your spouse's behavior.

Here is an example: if you had a harsh father who often scared you with his raging behavior, you may fear expressing your needs to your husband because you have been conditioned to expect a man to rage at you. You may have a very gentle husband, but if he raises his voice even slightly, you begin bracing yourself for the storm you expect. The ghost in your interaction with your husband is your father.

Another example: your mother may have been very dependent on your father and later she depended on you so much that even as a young adult, you didn't know that it was normal for you to separate from your mother to create a family of your own. You grew to think of your mother, who for you was the symbol of "woman" (and consequently all women) as a dependent, manipulative woman who drained you and yet still kept demanding more.

Even though you married a woman who is not like your mother, every time she asks something of you, your mother's ghost appears. You interpret your wife's normal request as manipulative and you respond to her as if she were acting like your mother did.

It is also possible and quite normal for you to have married someone very similar to one or both of your parents. Even if the behavior is similar, beware of the ghosts. If you develop a habit of making your spouse be a stand in for those ghosts, you are not interacting with your spouse. Instead you are talking to your ghosts!

Other ghosts of relationships past include former girlfriends, boyfriends, or spouses. When your spouse acts similarly to your ex, often your automatic response is to engage as if s/he were that ex.

Action step:

Do you want to stop talking to the Ghosts of Relationships Past? What's your first step? **Pay Attention and Be Aware.**

- ☐ Take inventory of your recent arguments with your spouse. Next do some archeological investigating into your past relationships. Where are the patterns?
- ☐ List the significant people in your past, including parents, siblings, and people with whom you have had a romantic relationship with.
- ☐ In your list, include the positive and negative interactions or behavioral patterns.
- ☐ Write your insights that you gain from doing this action step.
- ☐ How can you use what you just found out about yourself and your interactions with your ghosts that can help you in your present relationship?

Affirmation: I am aware of my Ghosts of Relationships Past. I strive to be curious and slow down before I react to my spouse as if s/he were one of my relationship ghosts.

> **16. The skills you learned as a child to protect yourself may not work and may actually be harmful in your adult relationships.**

When I was a child, around nine or 10 years old, I hated to be tickled. To this day I detest it. Often when the children were playing in our church recreation center someone got the bright idea that we should have a tickling free-for-all. As soon as I saw another child running toward me with his fingers extended, ready to tickle me, I panicked, turned tail, and fled.

Fortunately for me, I came up with a brilliant defense against tickling. I'd be minding my own business, playing with my friends, when someone would shout, "Tickle fight!" That was my signal to protect myself. I immediately found the nearest wall and squatted in front of it with my knees in front of my torso. I held my arms rigidly against my sides and scrunched my neck down as much as I could. I envisioned myself as a turtle going into its shell.

This tactic was extremely effective. If a child was running toward me and I hit the wall and went into my turtle stance, the child immediately gave up. It didn't take much to realize that I was too difficult of a target. So the child moved on quickly to find another victim to tickle.

This was my best and only defense against tickling and it worked perfectly. The other children could play their game and leave me out of it. I was proud of myself and my ability to protect myself from something I feared and despised.

I know that some children had to protect themselves from far more menacing threats. I will mention these horrors once again:

- ☐ Alcoholic parents
- ☐ Raging abusive parents
- ☐ Domestic violence between their parents or guardians
- ☐ Physical and sexual violence against them at home or from others who were supposed to be in charge of their safety and protection

- Many other frightening events over which the children had no control and no way to escape from

The effect of these experiences is that these children learned to protect themselves as best as they could. Whether your childhood was frightening and unsafe or you were presented with minor challenges like my tickling story, you still learned a lot in your childhood about how to protect yourself.

Some of those skills are still useful but others are not going to serve you well in your marriage. As a child you were vulnerable and so you figured out how to protect yourself as best as you could. As an adult in your marriage, when things get tense and you sense conflict coming on, you also want to protect yourself.

People do not like to feel vulnerable. However, if you cannot be open and let down your guard with your spouse, you shut out the possibility of true intimacy with the one you married. Your task is to learn some new skills so that you can allow yourself to be present in your marriage.

Here are some skills that a child may have used to feel safe that are counter-productive in intimate relationships:

- Passive-aggressive behavior: When children are not given permission to say "ouch" when offended or angry, they may transfer their angry feelings onto siblings, the family pet, or other children at school. They may figure out elaborate ways to get their siblings in trouble to deal with their "unacceptable" feelings.

There are many types of passive-aggressive behaviors. Here are two:

- Sarcasm: A child who was not allowed to express anger inappropriately (slamming doors, yelling, stomping, making a face) and was not given any skills for expressing anger appropriately (saying, "I'm mad" and being encouraged to talk about it, drawing a picture about the feelings, doing some exercise) may learn to use sarcasm as a means to express their feelings of anger.

- ☐ Silent treatment: Children figure out pretty quickly that this behavior is very effective. No one likes to be ignored or treated as if they were invisible. The child feels a sense of power when refusing to talk to the person s/he is angry with.

Anger doesn't go away just because the child is told that "anger is bad." It just changes form. Children do not have the ability to reason like adults do. Often, when the behavior works well, getting the results the child wants (attention, whether positive or negative; sympathy; a delay in bedtime), the child keeps using it and carries it into adulthood.

Just because you grow up doesn't mean you automatically gain adult relationship skills. If it's working, why change it, right? Well, it may work, but at the cost of good feelings, trust, and intimacy in your marriage.

Action step:

Here is a task for you to record in your journal:

- ☐ Ask yourself which childhood behaviors served you well as a child even if they got you in lots of trouble.
- ☐ Think about which of those behaviors you still use in times of stress. Yes, sometimes even grown ups throw tantrums.
- ☐ Pick one of those behaviors to start working on, especially if you know it is hurting your marriage.
- ☐ Make a plan to replace that behavior with another one that helps you calm yourself and works better when you are dealing with difficulties in your marriage.
- ☐ Use the tips and tools in this book to help you figure out what you are going to do instead.
- ☐ If you find you are unable to figure out how to shift out of your childhood behaviors, find someone to help you, such as a relationship coach or a therapist.

Affirmation: I now choose to learn how to modify my childhood coping skills to help me in my adult relationships.

Warning:

Are You Slipping Into the Danger Zone?

"Remember that the best relationship is one in which your love for each other exceeds your need for each other." Dalai Lama XIV

17. Silent treatment is a violation of your boundaries.

Remember John Gottman's Four Horsemen of the Apocalypse? One of the Horsemen is stonewalling. Stonewalling can also be called silent treatment. If it goes on for longer than a day, I call it a Silent Siege. If you have ever been the target of silent treatment by your spouse, you know how painful it can be. **If you choose stonewalling as a way of dealing with conflict, your relationship is in danger.**

Here are some behaviors you may have experienced as the target of a Silent Siege:

- ☐ Your spouse acts as if you do not exist, looking through you or making no eye contact at all.
- ☐ While your spouse is not talking to you s/he may talk with family members and friends as if nothing is wrong. This sends a crystal clear message that the Silent Siege is aimed specifically at you.
- ☐ You may attempt to engage your spouse and get a few monosyllables or nothing at all.
- ☐ Your spouse may avoid you by staying away physically or may remain in your home with you, but be so disconnected from you that s/he might as well be miles away.

How do you deal with the silent siege?

- ☐ You may cry, plead, and beg your spouse to talk to you.
- ☐ You may yell and curse, hoping to force your spouse to engage you.
- ☐ You may decide to retaliate and act the same way, which often leads to a power struggle to see who blinks first.
- ☐ You may isolate yourself from family and friends or do the opposite and tell everyone how awful your spouse is behaving.

If you are the one who uses silent treatment, here are a few ideas about why a Silent Siege may be a tool of choice for you:

- Conflict may stress you out to the point that you feel overwhelmed and helpless. You may feel the only thing you can do is retreat.
- You may feel increasingly stressed out and overloaded if your spouse tries to get you to talk and you may retreat further.
- You may feel like a victim and have no idea what to do.
- It feels good to have power and a Silent Siege gives you that power. You are withholding goodwill and affection from your spouse.
- It may be a way of punishing your spouse for what you think is misbehavior.
- Some people hold grudges for a very long time. Grudge holding may stem from a fear that if you "forgive" your spouse for behaviors you don't like, your spouse will continue to do those behaviors.

Keep in mind that keeping silent when overwhelmed is often a good idea. It helps you avoid saying something you will regret later. Continuing a Silent Siege for days or even weeks turns it into a different animal. If you use this particular method for dealing with conflict, I urge you to learn some new skills immediately. Silent Sieges can eventually lead to the destruction of your relationship.

What are the consequences of Silent Sieges on your marriage?

- Eroding of trust. It's hard to feel safe and comfortable with someone who withdraws physically and emotionally after a conflict for an extended period of time.
- A general atmosphere of fear and tension. You begin to tread on eggshells, even after the siege is over, wondering when the next Silent Siege will start.
- Laughter and easy conversation are replaced with stilted, generic talk about the weather. Other topics are soon deemed too dangerous, as they may bring on another Silent Siege.
- Avoidance and fear of bringing up what is bothering you.

- ☐ A conviction that you need to keep the peace at all costs. You may even deny that anything is bothering you if asked directly.
- ☐ Suppressing feelings of discomfort.
- ☐ Resentment, anger, and bitterness replace intimacy, love, joy and harmony.
- ☐ Intimacy dwindles. Spontaneous displays of affection, which were abundant when you first got together, slow down or disappear.
- ☐ You and your spouse may begin to "grow apart."

Action steps for the target of the Silent Siege:

If you have been the target of Silent Sieges in your marriage, here are a few things you might do to help yourself deal with this difficult behavior:

- ☐ I know it's hard to do, but I want you to practice acting "as if" your spouse is behaving normally. I don't mean pretend there is no problem. Greet your spouse as if s/he is not stonewalling. Talk in a normal tone of voice about normal, everyday things, as if you are both engaged in the conversation, even if you are the only one talking.
- ☐ Don't address the conflict that lead to your spouse's decision to stonewall. Resist the temptation to plead, cajole, or threaten your spouse to make her/him talk to you.
- ☐ Go about your normal routine. Reconnect with friends and family and spend time doing fun things with them. **Avoid isolation.**
- ☐ This is very important: take time to take care of yourself. Go to the movies, the bookstore, for daily walks, and so on. Caution: this does not mean going on an expensive shopping spree that will lead to more conflict later. Nor does it mean leaving town for several days to go on a private vacation without informing your spouse of your whereabouts.

- ☐ If repeated attempts to resolve a problem end up with the same stonewalling behavior from your spouse, perhaps it is best to let that particular grievance go, see a professional about the conflict, or find a way to find peace about the problem within yourself.
- ☐ When your spouse has decided to end the silent siege, please refrain from saying sarcastic things like, "It's about time you stopped pouting" or "I wondered when you'd finally get over yourself." That is, unless you want to continue the conflict.

Action steps for the stonewalling spouse:

If you have been using Silent Sieges in your marriage and you want to be a part of the solution, change this behavior as quickly as possible. You don't need weeks to figure things out and find a solution. If you want to break this very destructive habit, do it in small steps:

- ☐ Begin by telling your spouse that you need some time to think. Give an estimate of a few hours.
- ☐ Take those few hours to focus on how you can be a part of the solution. If you spend those hours focusing on nursing your hurt, recreating the argument, and placing blame on your spouse, you remain focused on the problem.
- ☐ Ask yourself what you can do to create harmony in your marriage.
- ☐ If you have no idea where to start, you might do well to hire a relationship coach or a marriage counselor.

Affirmation: I am willing to change the destructive habits in my marriage. I work on them in small steps and I forgive myself when I miss the mark, starting again to continue my progress. I ask for help when I need it.

18. Be careful about assuming that you know what your spouse is thinking and why your spouse acts a certain way.

Mind-reading is dangerous. Are you misreading the intentions of your spouse? Even if you've been together for decades, you are still not telepathic. You may be able to finish each other's sentences and you may be able to guess what your spouse is thinking many times, but you will still never be inside each other's heads. Thank goodness!

Of course, after a while you can learn to recognize certain non-verbal behaviors and see patterns. Hopefully, you have learned how to avoid saying things that hurt each other's feelings.

If you have been on the receiving end of your spouse's mind-reading, you know how frustrating it is to be told that you are doing a particular thing for a particular reason. Even if your spouse is 100% correct about your motivation, it still feels like a violation of your mind. If you tend to be the mind-reader, realize that even if you are right, you would do well to respect your spouse's boundary of what is inside his/her head.

Action step:

- ☐ Stay curious instead of jumping to conclusions. This will lead to a different outcome than your usual one.
- ☐ Turn assumptions into expectancy. The difference is that you are now expecting to hear the completion of your spouse's thoughts, rather than deciding you know what those thoughts are.

Affirmation: I let go of the need to mind-read. I stay in Curious Mode with my spouse.

> **19. Anger is only an emotion. However, anger becomes a toxic state if you linger there.**

Anger is an emotion that may come up quickly and end just as quickly. Anger is "a strong feeling of displeasure and belligerence aroused by a wrong." A grudge is different. A grudge is "a feeling of ill will or resentment." Anger is an automatic response, a feeling that comes up spontaneously when you are afraid of getting something you don't want, or not getting something you do want. What you do next with the angry feeling can have a profound effect on your relationship.

A grudge is a conscious choice. There is a reason why people use the phrase "nursing a grudge." When you hold onto anger and allow yourself to build up resentment, you are, indeed, nursing a grudge. You may believe that you have no choice in the matter. The longer you hold onto your feelings of ill will and resentment, the stronger your belief that you have no choice becomes.

Action step:

Are you willing to allow a grudge to come between you and the ones you love? If not, take steps now to reverse this bad habit. Start by asking yourself these questions and writing your answers in your journal.

- ☐ What is happening to my relationship as I continue to hold onto anger and resentment?
- ☐ What do I fear will happen if I let go of this grudge?
- ☐ Am I trying to teach the object of my grudge a lesson? If so, is it working? Is the lesson I'm trying to teach the message that is being received?
- ☐ What do I really want to have happen as a result of holding this grudge?
- ☐ Is there another way to get my needs met? Perhaps a gentler way that reconnects me with my spouse instead of one that punishes?

Affirmation: I acknowledge that anger is simply an emotion and I can choose how I express it. I seek new and helpful ways to express anger that reconnect me with my spouse.

20. Constructive criticism is an oxymoron.

No one enjoys criticism. Even supposed "constructive criticism" is often hard to hear. While some people can hear constructive criticism and learn from it, most people just get hurt, defensive, and sometimes downright angry. **Criticism destroys relationships.** You know what it's like to be on the receiving end of criticism and if you are like most people, you do not enjoy being criticized.

So what do you do if criticism is one of your frequent behaviors?

Action step:

- ☐ Your first task is to recognize a critical thought before it leaves your mouth in the form of the spoken word.
- ☐ Next, while the thought is still inside your head, ask yourself whether what you are thinking about is going to help or hurt your relationship.
- ☐ Finally, decide whether you can say it differently (more kindly, worded in a positive way) or whether you would be better off saying nothing at all.

Affirmation: I recognize critical thoughts before they become words. I choose my words carefully.

> **21. Comparing your spouse to others is as fun for her/him as it was when you were compared unfavorably to your siblings growing up.**

Joe walked out into the street and managed to get a taxi just going by. He got into the taxi, and the taxi driver said, "Perfect timing. You're just like Bryan."

"Who is that?" Joe asked.

The taxi driver responded, "Bryan Smith. There's a guy who did everything right. Like my coming along when you needed a cab. It would have happened like that to Bryan."

"There are always a few clouds over everybody," said Joe.

"Not Bryan. He was a terrific athlete. He could have gone on the pro tour in tennis. He could golf with the pros. He sang like an opera baritone and danced like a Broadway star," replied the taxi driver.

"He was something, huh?" said Joe.

"He had a memory like a steel trap. Remembered everybody's birthday. He knew all about wine, which fork to eat with. He could fix anything. Not like me. I change a fuse, and I black out the whole neighborhood," responded the taxi driver sadly.

"No wonder you remember him," Joe added sympathetically.

"Well, I never actually met Bryan," the taxi driver returned.

"Then how do you know so much about him?" asked Joe.

"Because I married his widow."

As a widow myself, I do find myself comparing my late husband to my new husband. I loved my late husband dearly and I grieved his death profoundly. I had just turned 40 years old when he died. I enjoyed my marriage with him, so I determined that I wanted to be happily married again and set out to find a new man with whom I could build a new life.

My new husband is definitely different than my late husband. This does not mean it's a bad thing, just different. While I do notice these differences and I do make comparisons, I also know better than to voice these comparisons, especially if they would only serve to make my new spouse look bad and feel bad.

Sometimes comparisons come in other forms. A husband may yell at his wife, "You're just like your mother," which can lead to nothing good, since it is usually not meant as a compliment. A wife may tell her husband, "You're just like your no good brother."

As a child, you may have dreaded and resented those negative comparisons to your siblings or other children:

- ☐ Why can't you get good grades like your sister does?
- ☐ Your brother behaves at the dinner table and eats all his vegetables (implying that you should, too).
- ☐ You should practice the piano more. Then you might be as good as the other students.

No one enjoys being compared unfavorably to someone else. If you want to keep your marriage strong and healthy, avoid the temptation to try to fix your husband by saying, "Jenny's husband mows the lawn every Saturday. Why can't you?"

If you want to preserve the close, loving feelings, do not tell your wife, "Why can't you make a pot roast like my mother does?"

Action step:

Focus instead on what you do like about your spouse and tell her/him often. The more you do this the more you create loving feelings toward each other. If you want changes, you can ask for them without comparisons:

- ☐ "Honey, I would like the lawn to be mowed more regularly. If you are not willing or able to do it weekly, can we hire someone to do it on the weeks you cannot?" is a start in the right direction.
- ☐ "Dear, I love your cooking. I especially love the way you make your delicious chicken casserole. I have a request. I miss some of the foods my mom used to make. Would you be willing to talk with my mom about how she makes her pot roast or ask her for the recipe?" This is a much more loving way to ask for what you want.

Affirmation: Instead of negative comparisons, I choose to focus on what I love about my spouse.

Power Struggles:

Do You Want to Be Right or in Harmony?

"The meeting of two personalities is like the contact of two chemical substances: if there is any reaction, both are transformed."
Carl Gustav Jung

> **22. Power struggles keep you on the Hamster Wheel of Conflict.**

Power struggles result when you (or your spouse) want something different than what is happening in your marriage. Sometimes these struggles stem from childhood expectations (that's how we always did it when I was growing up). Sometimes they come from deeply embedded insecurities.

Other sources of stress include overwork, childrearing, financial difficulties, jealousy, illness or injury, taking care of elderly parents, family conflicts, unemployment, and the list goes on. It's easy for power struggles to erupt when dealing with additional stressors.

What is the nature of your particular power struggle?

Is it relatively simple, such as how to distribute household chores? Is it more complex, such as asking for a major behavioral change from your spouse (or anything in the list above)?

When you and your spouse are locked in a power struggle, take a break and do some work by yourself, writing your answers in your journal.

- ☐ First, define the problem as you see it. Get detailed. If you think things should be different, describe why you believe this.
- ☐ If you feel a vague sense of discomfort, explore that feeling until you can figure out what is bothering you. Asking your spouse for a behavioral change based on a vague feeling is not enough unless your spouse is unusually compliant. Even an extremely easy-going person will eventually feel resentment if s/he is asked to change for undefined reasons.

As you explore your thoughts and feelings, make an agreement with yourself that you will be open to the possibility that you are asking for something based solely on your preference and not something that is "life or death."

Action step:

Ask yourself these questions and write your answers in your journal:

- ☐ What do I believe are my rights in my marriage?
- ☐ What is the worst thing that will happen if my spouse does not modify her/his behavior to my liking?
- ☐ Is my request reasonable? (if it's based on fears and insecurities, you may need to do some soul-searching. This may be more about you than about your spouse's behavior)
- ☐ Is what my spouse doing immoral, illegal, unethical, or harmful?
- ☐ Do I trust my spouse?
- ☐ If I do not trust my spouse, when did I decide to give up trusting my spouse? Was it connected to a particular event? Is it related to my Ghosts of Relationships Past?
- ☐ Is my spouse capable of making choices with the best interest of the relationship in mind?
- ☐ Does my spouse generally make choices with the best interest of our relationship in mind?

Affirmation: My spouse is my friend. I trust my spouse. I let go of the need to have constant power struggles with my spouse.

23. Marriage counseling isn't about fixing your spouse.

"When I focus on me, the blessing that comes is incredible clarity in my relationship to others. When I focus on you, I stay in a state of confusion." Joan Ellis

If you go into marriage therapy hoping to convince the counselor that your spouse is a broken person who needs to be fixed, I suggest you save your money. A good therapist avoids playing judge. There are three parts to every marriage: yours, your spouse's, and the relationship itself. I tell my clients, "I am not on your or your spouse's side. I am on the side of the relationship."

This is not to say that I will not notice the behaviors of both spouses. I notice defensiveness, sarcasm, blaming statements, critical talk, and other destructive behaviors coming from each spouse. It's my training to notice these things. I definitely raise a mental eyebrow when I ask my clients to look at their own troubling behaviors and one of the spouses will say, "I don't do any of that."

I usually reply that everyone who is breathing has engaged in negative, destructive behaviors toward those they love. Some people are not ready to do the work of self-examination. If your spouse is that person, you can still work on your own behavior. Neither you nor a therapist or relationship coach is going to be able to penetrate the defenses of someone who is not ready or willing to do this work.

If they are ready and willing to follow through on the action plan we create together, I can help my clients get off the Merry-Go-Round of Blame, breaking the cycle that keeps them going round and round in circles.

Action step:

☐ If you are focused on fixing your spouse, let this go. You have a lifetime's worth of work ahead of you with your own self-growth journey.

Affirmation: I know that by focusing on my own behavior I can help myself grow. In doing this I am able to improve my marriage.

24. Score-keeping is great when you are in competitive sports. It's counterproductive in your marriage.

If you maintain that you are going to refuse to work on your behavior unless your spouse is onboard and working on his/hers, you are playing a dangerous game of score keeping. You are within your rights to demand that your spouse do her/his share, but you are not likely to "win the relationship" if you insist on cooperation when your spouse is unwilling to give it to you, or unable to comply in the way you want.

It's easy to get discouraged when you are having conflicts in your marriage. It's also easy to reward your spouse for his/her progress by working on your own (and to stop working on your progress if s/he doesn't do the agreed upon work).

When you hold your accountable behavior hostage, refusing to work on yourself until your spouse gets with the program, you are guilty of rewarding to control your spouse's behavior. An example of rewarding is doing something for your spouse, but only if s/he does something for you. In this case, you may say, "Why should I work on improving my behavior if s/he is doing nothing?"

My answer to you is, "Why should you not?" What has your spouse's self-improvement got to do with your decision to work on yourself? You have an opportunity to shift your relationship just by doing your own work. When you change your behavior the relationship changes and the way you relate to each other changes. It happens automatically as you learn and grow, and you affect each other through your new and improved ways of interacting with each other.

Your progress will not be in a straight line. Be patient and kind to yourself and to each other. I cannot emphasize this enough!

You have enough to do by turning inward and focusing on your own self-improvement to last you for the rest of your life. I don't say this to make you think you are so messed up that you will spend the rest of your life fixing your broken self. No, this is true of everyone, including me! Every time I recognize that I am going into my default, "fix my husband" mode, I realize that I must shift out of that and into looking at my own behavior and what I can do to help my relationship.

It is natural for you to want your spouse to be on the same page and to work on her/his own self-growth at the same time you are. It is also natural to cajole her/him into action. While it is natural, it is counterproductive and often destructive, frequently eroding the good feelings you have for each other.

You know how you get when people try to force you to do something that you don't want to do? You may eventually do it, but you will drag your feet and protest loudly. It's also likely that you will begin to resent the person who is insisting that you toe the line. Eventually you may thank that person for having insisted that you do what you didn't want to do. Or not.

Action step:

- ☐ Acknowledge that you are human and like everyone else, you can fall into the trap of score-keeping.
- ☐ Resist the temptation to focus on what your spouse is or is not doing.
- ☐ Keep track of the work you are doing toward your own self-growth in your journal.
- ☐ Measure your progress against what you have already done. Think of it like a growth chart for a child. You measure the child's growth against the last measurement, not against another child's growth.

Affirmation: I let go of scorekeeping in my marriage. We are on the same team!

25. Unrealistic expectations can wreak havoc in your relationship.

Many people are unhappily married. Could it be that their expectations are unrealistic?

Children get ideas about what marriage is suppose to be like by watching their parents, other adults, and seeing depictions of relationships in the movies and on television. Sometimes these examples are helpful and other times they set people up for totally unrealistic expectations for marriage.

When I was growing up, I remember watching movies and television and thinking that people met and had sex after knowing each other only a few hours. I had no idea what "sex" was even in my teens. I was quite sheltered. "Sex" in my innocent mind meant kissing and lying in bed with no clothes on.

These were messages I was getting from the media despite my mother's best efforts to shield me from negative influences. Before you start thinking my childhood was racy, I wasn't watching rated R movies! This was on mainstream television in the 1970's and 1980's when I was a child. There was nothing graphic, but the message was clear.

As a result, I thought this was what couples were "supposed" to do when they first met, which clashed with what I was being taught in Sunday school. It was quite confusing. I was given certain values and expectations about marriage from my parents and my religious upbringing. Television and movies presented a completely different message.

Maybe you can relate. Here are some other unrealistic expectations I received from a variety of sources during my early years:

- ☐ Someday my prince will come (from fairy tale books).
- ☐ Along with the prince fantasy, I grew up hearing that there was one special person out there just for me (a soul mate).

- ☐ Marriage would make me happy.
- ☐ My spouse was supposed to make me happy.
- ☐ My task as a wife was to make my spouse happy.
- ☐ Everything will work out fine as long as you have good chemistry/good values/put God first, etc.
- ☐ I'm supposed to be the number one priority in my spouse's life.
- ☐ My spouse and I will always agree (or we will rarely argue).

As you can see, when I was growing up, I really didn't understand much at all about successful relationships, despite my parents' best efforts. If you are reading this and nodding your head, then you know what I'm talking about! Fortunately, I made it my mission to figure out how to create successful relationships and to share my knowledge with others. It has taken a long time and I will tell you that unrealistic expectations are often like weeds. They are very hard to get rid of! But not impossible.

You can often spot these unrealistic expectations when you are feeling like something is not fair or "should" be a certain way. When you notice this feeling, test your thought. Chances are, you are dealing with an unrealistic expectation.

Action step:

- ☐ Write your unrealistic expectations about relationships in your journal.
- ☐ Ask yourself where these expectations came from: childhood, observing parents or other adults in relationships, the media (news, television, books, movies, music, and so on).
- ☐ Challenge these unrealistic expectations, rewriting them into more realistic ones. An example would be writing "Marriage is supposed to make me happy" (unrealistic). Rewritten it might read "Marriage can be happy and it is up to me to create a loving environment in which we can experience joy together."

Affirmation: I recognize the unrealistic expectations that I have been fed since childhood. I work toward creating a happy marriage with more realistic expectations.

26. "Should" is a four letter word.

I rank the word "should" right up there with curse words. Sometimes you may be using "should" to make your spouse do something you want done. Sometimes you are "shoulding" on yourself.

- ☐ You should treat me better.
- ☐ You should take me out to eat.
- ☐ I should be a better person.
- ☐ I should be able to understand this.

Should is a word I would love for you to take out of your vocabulary. It is a word used to shame yourself or your spouse into doing what you want done or what you think ought to be done.

What would work better?

Requesting a behavioral change instead of demanding it is a good start. Being kinder to yourself instead of "shoulding" on yourself is another way to deal with your desire to improve.

Requesting a behavioral change:

- ☐ I would prefer that you treat me this way (get specific with what you **DO** want instead of what you do not want).
- ☐ I would love to go out to eat with you (instead of "You never take me out to eat. You should take me to dinner.").

For your self-talk:

- ☐ I am a work in progress and I strive to improve myself with small steps.
- ☐ I don't understand this right now and that is all right. I'm working on understanding (or I can ask for help if I don't understand).

Action step:

If you find that you often use words like "should" or "ought" or "must" take a break to examine what is behind those words. Ask yourself these questions:

- ☐ Am I trying to control my spouse by declaring that s/he "should" do what I say?
- ☐ Who says my spouse "should" do what I want? Why "should" this be true?
- ☐ Is it working to shame my spouse (or myself) by saying that s/he "should" do what I want? Is it getting the results I want **and** keeping the harmony in my relationship?
- ☐ How can I ask for what I need or want without using the word "should"?

Affirmation: I ask for what I need directly. I act with kindness toward my spouse and toward myself.

27. Marriages should be 50/50, right?

Who came up with this saying? It is thrown around as a "truth" so often that people believe it. I have seen some couples argue for years because, since they both work, they believe that both should do half of the household chores. The problem is everything is half done because of the way they've organized it.

If you do half a job, you haven't completed it. If you decide, without consulting your spouse, that s/he is supposed to do the other half, that's a recipe for constant conflict.

If you're putting 50% of your energy into your relationship, you're only doing half of what you need to do. Think about this: if you took a test with 100 questions and answered 50 of them correctly, you scored 50%. If you recall the grading system when you were in school, answering 50% of the questions correctly on a test gets you a failing grade.

Why is this 50/50 idea so prevalent when it comes to something as important as your marriage? If you look back at the example of doing half a chore, expecting your spouse to do the other half, it begins to look suspiciously like score-keeping:

- ☐ I washed the dishes, so you have to put them away.
- ☐ I cooked, so you have to clean.
- ☐ I cleaned the bathroom last week; it's your turn this week.

Then it turns into:

- ☐ If you're not going to take out the trash, then I'm not going to vacuum the living room.
- ☐ You didn't make the bed, so why should I pick my clothes off the floor?

What's the solution?

Action step:

- ☐ Be responsible for what you decide to do regardless of how your spouse behaves. This keeps you in integrity with yourself. Otherwise, you reduce your marital state to petty schoolyard behavior.
- ☐ Decide that you will do 100% of what you agree to do. Do it regardless of what your spouse does or does not do.

Refuse to settle for a failing grade in your marriage. Go for the 100% and you will find you have a much different marriage than those who believe in 50/50 relationships!

Affirmation: I let go of the need to keep score. I focus on my task of creating a happy relationship, not on whose turn it is to do something.

28. Anger is a "get my way" behavior.

If you recognize that you use anger to get your way, are you ready to do something different? If you are, decide to look at the situation as having many different possible solutions. Remember, your way is not the only way.

If you tend to argue just to win the argument, you can look forward to a lonely life. If you're in a relationship, you will spend a lot of time feeling miserable and blaming your spouse if you fight to win. Ask yourself if continued conflict is worth the toll it is taking on your marriage. Decide what you want to do instead.

Usually, when you want something done your way and you throw in the word "should" you are expressing a belief. Just because you believe something should be done a certain way doesn't make it true. If you begin dictating how your spouse should behave, s/he will resist. No one likes to be controlled.

Does your happiness really depend on what your spouse does or does not do? Think about it. If you really believe this, you are saying you are a helpless victim and your happiness is totally dependent on your spouse doing everything just the way you want it. Choose instead to take responsibility for what you can control: your own behavior.

Your task is to figure out ways to solve the problem. Agree to set aside some time for you and your spouse to brainstorm some options. They can be wild, far out ideas; it doesn't matter. You want to generate many possible ways to solve the problem. Be careful that your solutions don't start with what your spouse should do. Keep the focus on personal responsibility. Write at the top of a piece of paper the words "I can" and then list the things you can do to solve the problem.

Ask yourself how you can be a part of the solution. This is taking personal responsibility. It's a good idea to have this question at the front of your mind at all times. When you take personal responsibility, it's very hard for you to blame your partner.

"Don't sweat the small stuff...and it's all small stuff." Richard Carlson.

Remember that? You only have a short period of time to live your life. Do you want to spend your life in conflict? Do you want to spend your life being jerked around by your ego? Or would you rather spend your time wisely, connecting with the people you love?

"Let It Go" is a phrase I want you to keep in mind. Decide what you can accept and let the rest go. So many things are trivial until we make them important. You can choose harmony with your loved one. You can **choose flexibility** and watch conflict disappear.

Action step:

When your thoughts are leading you in the direction of anger, stop and ask yourself the following questions:

- ☐ Do I want to win the argument or win the relationship?
- ☐ What rule states that someone else "should" do what I want?
- ☐ Is it really true that my happiness depends on what my loved one does or doesn't do?
- ☐ What are some options to solve this problem?
- ☐ How can I be a part of the solution?
- ☐ In the grand scheme of things, how important is this?
- ☐ Can I decide to Let it Go?

Affirmation: I let go of the "small stuff," remembering that "it's all small stuff." I choose to be a part of the solution.

29. I have a right to let my anger out or I'll get an ulcer. Is this true?

Do you believe that if you don't express the anger you feel that you will explode? Some people believe that **NOT** expressing anger is harmful to them. Perhaps they got the message sometime in their lives that "stuffing" anger leads to depression, or ulcers, or an eventual explosion. I know this is a popular idea in my line of work and I have worked with plenty of clients who believed this.

I also know that I don't buy it and here's why: usually when people believe they have a right to let their anger out, what they often mean is "I have a right to rant and rave and shout at you or anyone else in my path." If they are angry, they believe their state of "upset" gives them the right to take it out on anyone and everyone.

For example: Tim is angry about how long it is taking for the waitress to bring his food, so he feels justified shouting at the waitress about how slow she is and about how the service of the restaurant is the worst he's experienced in years. It doesn't matter that it's a very popular restaurant and he is eating during the lunch hour, which is typically a very busy time of day. It doesn't matter that the waitress has no control over how long it takes the cooks to prepare the meal.

This type of behavior stems from a sense of entitlement. Tim is using anger as a "get my way" behavior.

Action step:

If you recognize your own "get my way" behavior here and you realize that you are harming people you love, and possibly even strangers, you're off to a great start. If you want to change this behavior, even better! Breaking an anger habit will take some time, but benefits to yourself and your relationships will amaze you!

- ☐ Learn to recognize the signals your body gives you when you feel angry. Some possible signs are tightness in your muscles, clenching of the jaw, stomach churning, and headaches.

- ☐ Create a plan to slow yourself down when you notice your body's signals. Some people take a break for 10 minutes. Others do physical exercise. Sometimes slowly sipping a glass of water helps. Here are a few other things people do to help them slow down when they notice they are feeling angry: prayer, meditation, deep breathing, yoga, and guided relaxation techniques.
- ☐ When you feel angry and you tell yourself that you have a right to "let it all out" ask yourself, "Is that true?"
- ☐ If you answer with a quick, "Of course it's true," follow up with, "Can I be absolutely certain that it's true?" and "How would someone I trust answer this question?"
- ☐ The most important thing is to slow yourself down or take yourself out of that situation if at all possible so that you can allow yourself to reflect in a quiet place.

Affirmation: I know it is all right to experience and express anger. I choose to learn new, helpful ways to express anger that do not harm others.

> **30. When you become stuck in the "fix it" role, it creates an imbalance in your relationship, leading to resentment by both parties.**

Many women believe that men, being natural problem-solvers (biologically based), are guilty of trying to fix things more often than women. It's safe to say that both sexes are guilty of engaging in "fix it" behavior.

Why do you try to fix things?

- ☐ You may believe you are doing the right thing.
- ☐ You may feel a sense of obligation (or even guilt) to help.
- ☐ You may believe that a good person *should* help.

What do all of these beliefs do **for** you and **to** you? Best case scenario: you feel a sense of satisfaction at having helped someone else, especially if things work out well. Often, however, the opposite is more likely:

- ☐ The one you are helping may feel resentful.
- ☐ You may feel resentful that you "have to" help.
- ☐ The one who is receiving the help may feel guilty that s/he could not do it alone.
- ☐ The one you help may become more helpless and even more dependent on your aid.
- ☐ You may both begin to feel stuck in this negative cycle.

If you would like to change this pattern, instead of immediately offering to help, slow yourself down. Start by finding out more about the situation. It is very possible that your spouse wants to solve the problem alone or with minimal guidance or assistance. Maybe your spouse only wants a second opinion. By pausing to evaluate the situation, you allow yourself to stop automatically fixing things. You also allow your spouse to come up with the solution that works best for her/him. After all, you married a capable person, right?

Action step:

If your spouse is looking at you to rescue her/him or fix the problem, first ask your spouse a series of questions:

- ☐ What have you done so far?
- ☐ What is the next step?
- ☐ What do you think the problem is?
- ☐ What do you think will help you solve this?
- ☐ Where do you want to go with this?
- ☐ End with: Let me know how it works out.
- ☐ If you can think of a suggestion that will help, ask: Could I offer a suggestion? (if the answer is no, leave it alone)

If you can offer a name or telephone number of a helpful person, agency, or reference, do this. You will find yourself less resentful when you let go of your role as "Fix it Person." If your spouse (or other family members) have expected you to fix things for them for a very long time, it may be difficult at first to get out of this role. Keep in mind that it's not easy to change long-standing patterns, yet it is possible.

Affirmation: I enjoy helping others when I can and I now know that I can step back and allow others, especially my spouse, to solve problems without my help (or interference).

31. There are so many "right" ways to do things; don't quibble over doing it "your" way.

If you often say to yourself, "I have to do everything around here," ask yourself why you say that. I've worked with many clients who have said this to me and what I discovered is that they have some exacting standards. The dishes must be cleaned in just a certain way, the socks have to be folded just so, the toilet paper must go on the holder just the way they want it, and so on.

What does this mean? Control. Lots of it. Behind the control is the belief that there is only one right way to do something. I confess that I'm a recovering Control Freak, so I know what I'm talking about!

The problem with control is that you exhaust yourself trying to nag others into doing it the "right" way, or in redoing it when they haven't done it to your satisfaction. What's worse is you have trained your spouse and family to give up and stop doing anything since they cannot do things to your satisfaction. Or they may do things your way but rest assured that they resent you for it!

Action step:

Here are some questions to ask yourself when you feel compelled to make someone do it your way:

- ☐ Who says my way is the best way?
- ☐ Where did my belief that things have to be done in just a certain way come from?
- ☐ What do I gain from holding onto the belief that my way is the best way? What do I lose?
- ☐ Is this belief worth holding onto?
- ☐ What is the worst thing that will happen if I let go and allow others to do it their way in their own time?

Experiment with letting go of the need to have things done your way. You will probably find that the house may not be as clean or tidy as you want it to be. The children may not be dressed the way you want or have their homework done according to your time structure. Can you live with that? If your answer is, "No, I cannot," ask yourself the Action Step questions again.

Look at your options, which may include:

- ☐ Continuing to do it all yourself
- ☐ Hiring someone to help
- ☐ Setting more realistic standards
- ☐ Letting other family members help and being okay with the results (hey, it got done and it's one less thing you have to do)

Affirmation: My way is just one of many ways to do things. That's all right by me.

Your Beliefs:

What Do You Believe In?

"There are no facts, only interpretations." Friedrich Nietzsche

32. Your thoughts create your feelings.

For some people, the idea that what they think affects how they feel is a strange concept. What is more comfortable is that someone else "made" them angry or upset.

Think about this:

Suppose that when you first wake up in the morning you notice it is raining. Your first thought is, "Ugh. I don't want to get out of bed. The traffic is going to be crazy. People don't know how to drive in the rain." When you finally drag yourself out of bed, you are already feeling tense and perhaps irritable because you are facing some heavy traffic with incompetent drivers.

I like the expression "Never judge a day by the weather." What if you decided to cancel your original thought and instead said, "It's raining. My drive to work will probably be longer so I'll take one of my favorite pieces of music to listen to while I drive." How different does that thought feel?

In the first scenario you ended up feeling stressed and tense because of what you told yourself immediately upon awakening. In the second one you changed your thoughts and ended up with calmer feelings.

Action step:

You cannot simply get rid of negative thoughts. Instead, replace them with more helpful thoughts.

- ☐ Notice your negative thoughts and the feelings that result from those thoughts.
- ☐ Say, "Cancel that."
- ☐ Choose some new thoughts that are more helpful.
- ☐ Notice how you feel once you replace the negative thoughts with positive ones.

Affirmation: I notice when my thoughts are negative and I immediately change them around to something more positive. I feel myself shift into better feelings when I do this.

33. Your opinion is a belief, and may not even be yours to begin with.

Byron Katie has written some wonderful books about changing your beliefs around thoughts that are making you miserable. She has a concept she calls The Work. In it she asks some profound questions to help you examine your beliefs. Your beliefs about a situation or a person can create stressful thoughts. Katie maintains that your stressful thoughts are what cause misery, not the situation itself.

This may be a bitter pill to swallow if you keep looking for a solution outside of yourself. If, on the other hand, you are willing to take personal responsibility and examine the unhelpful beliefs, it can be quite liberating. The answers are within you if you are ready to do some self-examination.

Action step:

- ☐ Whenever you have a stressful thought about your spouse (or anything), talk back to it.
- ☐ Ask yourself if you can be 100% certain, beyond a reasonable doubt, that your belief is actually true. Often, if you are honest with yourself, you will find that what you believe to be true is not as true as you originally thought.
- ☐ If you were to choose to let go of this particular belief, how would you be different? Who would you be if you got rid of this belief?

Affirmation: I am open to examining my beliefs that cause me stress. I remind myself that often what I believe is my opinion and not necessarily true.

> **34. If you are willing to reexamine your beliefs that you're sure are "facts" you can open up some new doors in your relationships.**

I often tell my clients, "Opinions are not facts." Just because you believe something strongly doesn't make it "the truth." Don't be so sure that what you think is a fact. Your opinions can get you in trouble when you label them as "the truth."

The American Heritage dictionary defines a **fact** as "knowledge or information based on real occurrence, something demonstrated to exist or known to have existed, or a real occurrence; an event."

In contrast, a **belief** is "the mental act, condition, or habit of placing trust or confidence in another, mental acceptance of and **conviction in the truth**, actuality, or validity of something, something believed or accepted as true, especially a particular tenet or a body of tenets accepted by a group of persons."

I have met people who do not believe that men landed on the moon. Others do not believe that dinosaurs were real. So there are times when people's beliefs run contrary to what people consider facts in general.

I'm not talking about extremes. I'm just asking you to be aware of things you believe so strongly that may or may not be factual. Often your beliefs are stories you have told yourself for so long that they feel like facts. Please understand that I am NOT referring to religious beliefs. I'm talking about beliefs you may have such as "men are only interested in sex" or "all women are terrible drivers" which are not facts, but rather stereotypes, generalizations, biases, or even prejudices.

Action step:

- ☐ When you feel something very strongly, you engage in "emotional reasoning." For example: "I feel bad, so my spouse must have made that comment to hurt me on purpose."
- ☐ If you're not sure which beliefs you hold that are not necessarily "facts," I ask you to start paying attention to what you are thinking. Soon you'll come across a belief that needs examining.

Affirmation: I am becoming more self-aware. I am careful to distinguish between beliefs and facts.

> **35. Sometimes people believe that a saying is true just because they've heard it so many times.**

You have heard many refrains so often that you don't even question them. Everyone has. Here are some examples of expressions you may have accepted as gospel truth without even stopping for a moment to determine whether they ring true for you:

- ☐ Things are going to get worse before they get better.
- ☐ Bad luck comes in threes.
- ☐ Life is hard and then you die.
- ☐ It's all downhill after the honeymoon is over.
- ☐ Marriage is hard work.
- ☐ Men and women will never understand each other.
- ☐ All the good ones are married (to someone else).
- ☐ A day that starts out bad will only get worse.
- ☐ Money can't buy happiness (therefore, rich people must be miserable).

Says who? Why should that be true? What if your **expectations** create the very thing you fear?

Action step:

- ☐ I challenge you be wary about accepting something you hear without questioning it. Examine these sayings and see if they are really true.

I don't expect you to agree with everything I say. My hope for you is that you will begin to live an aware life. You don't have to become a fanatic about it.

☐ Begin by gently noticing what rings true for you and what doesn't. This is enough to increase your awareness and to begin the process of living an aware life.

Affirmation: I now recognize sayings that I used to believe automatically. Now I question whether they are really true before I decide whether to believe them.

The Story
You're Telling Yourself About Your Situation Creates Your Happiness...or Misery

"Thoughts are things, and what you choose to focus on becomes real. Therefore, happiness - or misery - is a choice. What do you choose?"
Kim M. Baldwin

36. The story you're telling yourself about your situation may be keeping you stuck in bitterness and resentment.

Even if you have "good reason" to feel bitter and resentful, those feelings are not helping you. Also, if you're not honest with yourself, you cannot be absolutely sure the story you have been telling yourself is the "truth." It is what you **believe**, but there is no way to know if it is the absolute truth.

Bitterness keeps you stuck in your story. I encourage you to examine your current story and create a new story for yourself. Otherwise, you continue to believe something about yourself and those around you that keeps you stuck.

I want to add that other people's stories about you have nothing to do with you. Your story is what you tell yourself about your life, your actions, your beliefs and values (which are often not truly yours, but have been handed down to you). Socrates said, "An unexamined life is not worth living." You make your beliefs and values your own by examining them to make sure they fit for you.

Your story is also what you tell yourself about others. No one can ever really know another person completely. You can only know the story you tell yourself about that person, and often your story about others can use a lot of updating. Your story may be stuck in the last decade or two. Other people's stories about you may also be stuck, which is why some people may still see you the way they did when you were a child. People do grow and change!

"Listening to both sides of a story will convince you that there is more to a story than both sides." Frank Tyger

Action step:

- ☐ Examine your story. Write your observations in your journal. What do you believe about your situation that is giving you problems?
- ☐ The beliefs that are causing problems may not be "true." Ask yourself what other possible interpretations there are for your situation.
- ☐ Ask yourself what your life would be like if you decided to give up or modify the beliefs that are keeping you stuck.
- ☐ Based on your self-reflections, write your new story in your journal. Take your time. You don't have to write it all in one setting.
- ☐ Examine your story periodically and update it as needed.

As you learn and grow you are creating your new story!

Affirmation: I now decide to let go of the beliefs that are keeping me stuck. I am replacing these beliefs with more helpful ones.

37. If you're pessimistic about your marriage, be careful about creating a self-fulfilling prophesy.

Henry Ford said, "Whether you think you can or can't, you're right." Similarly, if you think your marriage is doomed, you are right. If you think your marriage is salvageable (or even blessed) you are right about that also. What you think about comes about, so be careful to monitor your persistent thoughts about your marriage.

Action step:

Notice your **persistent** thoughts. Don't get bogged down in fleeting thoughts. Fleeting thoughts are just that, fleeting, and they will pass. What you want to be concerned about are the persistent pessimistic thoughts that plague you. Now, do a test with a few questions which come from Cognitive Behavioral Therapy:

- ☐ Where's the evidence that my thought is true?
- ☐ Where's the evidence that my thought is false?
- ☐ What is another opinion (or what would someone else say)?
- ☐ What do I want to think and do based on this new assessment?
- ☐ As a result of thinking differently and doing something differently, how do I want to feel?

Schedule a time to write out these thoughts in your journal and challenge them by asking these five questions. You don't have to write them out every single time you have the thought. Decide on regular times to write, whether you do it daily, several times a week, or whenever the spirit moves you. The important thing is that you actively challenge these pessimistic thoughts so you can create newer, more helpful ones.

Affirmation: I am kind to myself as I lovingly examine and challenge these pessimistic thoughts and create more helpful ones.

38. How you choose to interpret someone's behavior affects how you feel about that person.

Okay, it *is* true. Sometimes people can be mean, and petty, and even malicious. Most of the time people just do what they do, though, without regard to how it impacts others. My late husband used to get angry at drivers who would cut him off, drive slowly in the passing lane, or do other stupid things that frustrated him. I would say, "Al, it's not about you. They are self-absorbed and not doing it to irritate you."

Similarly, when you assign meaning to your spouse's behavior, it affects how you feel about your spouse. Let's just say your husband leaves his dirty socks in the living room. You may think, "He doesn't care about me. He doesn't think about how this makes me feel." Most likely you would be right about the part about his not thinking about how it makes you feel. He may have no idea. He wasn't doing anything purposefully to **make** you feel bad. He was just doing what he does, which is taking off his socks. **It had nothing to do with you.**

"But," you say, "I've told him a hundred times to put his socks in the hamper and he still won't do it."

Again, unless you have married a vicious, malicious person who enjoys tormenting you, it's not about you. Of course, this may become a negative cycle, where the more you nag him about the socks the more he chooses to leave them lying around on the living room floor. That's a whole different situation.

But let's focus on the original point, which is that the story you are telling yourself about your spouse's behavior affects how you feel about him. You are creating stress for yourself with your **interpretation** of why he leaves the socks on the floor.

Action step:

Using the example of the socks on the floor, I ask you to play a game. The next time this happens, do the following:

- ☐ Notice your immediate reaction.
- ☐ Think or say out loud, "This behavior has nothing to do with me." Don't say it aloud with the intention of having your spouse hear you. Saying things aloud reinforces them in your mind; this is a tool for you, not for your spouse.
- ☐ Add to this, "There is no story here. This is simply one of my spouse's behaviors."

Affirmation: I let go of the story I've been telling myself about my spouse that is causing me misery. I choose to create a newer, more helpful story instead.

39. What you focus on increases. Are you focusing on positive or negative things?

Whatever you focus upon, increases. When you focus on the things you need, you'll find those needs increasing. A grateful perspective brings happiness and abundance into a person's life." Andy Andrews

When I first got my Honda Accord in 1999, I began to notice other cars just like mine everywhere. Where were they before? They were already out there, but I didn't notice them until I was focused on them. The more focused I became, the more I realized that Honda Accords were all around me. What I focused on increased, in a sense, if only in my awareness.

I wonder if it's "human nature" to focus on the negative. Perhaps it's just a bad habit, maybe one that was taught to us as children through what we heard our elders say. I'm pretty sure I confuse my clients when I ask them "What went right this week?" Most of the time people hire a counselor or relationship coach thinking they have to talk about problems. I shake things up when I ask about exceptions to the problem.

If you are focusing on what you do not want, what would happen if you turned it around and focused instead on what you DO want? I learned a long time ago that the brain cannot do a "not." For example, if you tell someone, "Don't think about pink elephants," they will immediately think about pink elephants. They cannot NOT think about them.

If you want to do or think something differently, you have to replace what you don't want with what you do want. That's why it's more helpful to tell running children "walking feet" instead of "don't run." The brain hears "run" and tells the body to keep going.

Action step:

- ☐ Notice when you are focusing on what you do NOT want.
- ☐ Ask yourself instead, "What DO I want?"
- ☐ Think about what happens when you get what you want. What do you do then?
- ☐ Here's an idea: just as you do with children, practice catching your spouse doing that thing you do want.
- ☐ Express your appreciation when you see what you want happening.

As you exercise this new habit of focusing on the positive, you will notice it increasing. You will notice that it happens more often.

Affirmation: I focus on the positive. I focus on what I do want and I notice more of it. I express appreciation when this happens.

Section Three:

Getting Back on The Happily Ever After Path

"It is only possible to live happily ever after on a day-to-day basis."
Margaret Bonanno

Personal Responsibility:

If It's To Be It's Up to Me

"Transformation isn't always comfortable and any time you are triggered, get upset or are angered, look at where the opportunity is for YOU to heal something in your life, i.e. an old belief that does not serve you." Kat Kirkwood, Life Transformation Coach

> **40. What small thing are you willing to do on a regular and consistent basis, regardless of what your spouse does or doesn't do, that you think will help your relationship?**

I am a big fan of Dr. William Glasser's Choice Theory and this is one of my favorite Choice Theory questions:

> What small thing are you willing to do
> on a regular and consistent basis,
> regardless of what your spouse does or doesn't do,
> that you think will help your relationship?

In my practice, my clients have often heard me ask them this very question. It's best to start with a small thing that you can do and build on it. Habits are built one behavior at a time. This is also true in relationships. I would love for you to begin the habit of asking yourself this powerful question.

When I ask my clients to think of one small thing they can do, I hand them a piece of paper with the Seven Deadly Habits of External Control on it to give them an idea of the behaviors that have been getting them in trouble.

The Seven Deadly Habits of External Control:

1. Criticizing
2. Blaming
3. Complaining
4. Nagging
5. Threatening
6. Punishing
7. Rewarding/bribing

If you are alive and breathing, you have done every one of these habits at some time or another. Confession time: my personal "favorite" deadly habits have been criticizing, blaming, and complaining. I've worked hard (and made pretty good progress) to reduce these deadly habits in my life, though I am human and I still have a way to go to get rid of them entirely.

Next, I show my clients the Seven Caring Habits, listed below. These are the habits I encourage them to use instead of the deadly ones.

Seven Caring Habits; the Mentally Healthy Alternative:

1. Supporting
2. Encouraging
3. Listening
4. Accepting
5. Trusting
6. Respecting
7. Negotiating Differences

Action step:

- ☐ Examine this list, decide which deadly habit you would like to work on first, and pick one aspect of this behavior to change. Keep it simple and small! If you tend to criticize, notice when you have a critical thought in your head and make a decision to do something different. It could be as simple as saying nothing. You could make a decision to rephrase or give words of praise for something else instead.
- ☐ Choose one of the caring habits and decide that you will practice this one habit to start with. You can pick one that you are already good at. Make it as easy as possible.
- ☐ Pick your small thing to do and get started today.

Affirmation: I choose helpful behaviors which make my marriage great every day.

> **41. If you spend a lot of your time complaining about your spouse to others, you're caught in the Complaint Trap!**

When I was in college I lived near my aunt Carrie and Uncle Jimmy. I would visit them often after classes and on weekends. A curious thing began to happen as I spent time alone with my aunt. She began to confide in me, as she never had before, about her marriage. I was 18 years old and this was quite strange to me.

She took every opportunity to complain about my uncle's behavior, giving me examples of things he did that aggravated her. They had been, I thought, happily married for almost 30 years at that time. I had never noticed any problems between them, so it was a bit disconcerting to hear my aunt complain about my uncle.

Being the naïve college freshman that I was, I gave her the only advice I could think of off the top of my head, which was, "If you don't like it, leave him." It was a very simplistic thing for me to say. I was in way over my head; believe it or not, I had no experience in listening to adults complain about their spouses.

What I didn't understand is that Aunt Carrie had no thought and no intention of leaving Uncle Jimmy; it wasn't part of the way she saw the world. Most of my relatives, including Carrie and Jimmy, believed in "till death do you part." Aunt Carrie and Uncle Jimmy lived together, happily or unhappily, until my uncle Jimmy died just after their 52nd wedding anniversary.

I don't know whether my Aunt Carrie was unhappy. I believe my aunt and uncle loved each other very much. I now realize that my aunt still has a habit of complaining about anything and everything. Despite this, I love her very much and still enjoy her company.

Complaining is one of the Seven Deadly Habits of External Control. It's one of the ways people attempt to feel better when they are not happy with something by trying to get **someone else** to do something different.

Sometimes people complain so frequently that they don't even notice anymore. Complaining has become an ingrained and automatic part of their everyday conversation.

If you have a habit of complaining to others about your spouse (or complaining to your spouse), it's time to examine this behavior. How does complaining help your marriage? Does it change your spouse's behavior toward you for the better? Does your spouse avoid you, fleeing from your litany of complaints?

Action step:

- ☐ Take a week's vacation from complaining. If you are a very skilled complainer, this may be hard for you.
- ☐ If a week is too difficult, start with a Complaint-Free Hour. Build on this challenge until you can spend a whole day free of complaints.
- ☐ Begin slowly by starting a journal of every complaint you make. Notice when your thoughts are complaints and write them down too. See how often you repeat yourself.
- ☐ As you begin to let go of the habit of complaining, write in your journal about the changes you notice in your marriage and other relationships.
- ☐ Write about what changes you notice in yourself.

Affirmation: I listen to my thoughts and if I hear a complaint, I easily shift into something more helpful. I am kind to myself as I learn new, more helpful ways to express myself.

42. Too many people would rather blame their ex than to look at the other person responsible for the demise of their relationship.

I know. Blame is easier than taking responsibility for the problems of a failed relationship. If you're honest with yourself, sometimes it even feels good. You feel vindicated. You tell your story about how awful your ex was and people sympathize with you.

Here's the problem with blame: it stunts your personal growth. You risk repeating the same patterns in yet another relationship. Sometimes it's not about you at all. Sometimes it's all about you. You may not be 100% responsible for the problems that result in the ending of a relationship, but you're not 100% blameless either.

If you want to get off the Bad Relationship Hamster Wheel, I encourage you to take a look at your own behavior, thoughts, and beliefs. This is a harder path, yet it is filled with rewards.

Once you understand yourself better and know why you act as you do, you are more likely to be able to choose better in your next relationship. You'll finally understand why you are attracted to a certain personality type. You'll be able to choose consciously instead of attracting someone who is all wrong for you by default. You'll be able to BE the person you want to attract. How cool is that?

Action step:

Use your journal to write about the beliefs you have had since you were a child. These are things your parents, teachers, or other people told you that were "true" that you accepted before you knew you could examine these beliefs and decide for yourself whether to accept them as yours.

Here are some questions to get you started:

- ☐ What were you told about how good girls and boys ought to behave?
- ☐ What did you learn from watching your parents or other adults that taught you about adult intimate relationships?
- ☐ If you had a parent who insisted that there was only one right way to do things, what did that teach you? What did you begin to believe?
- ☐ Spend some time thinking about what your past relationships taught you about yourself, your behaviors, and your choices.

My hope for you is that as you examine these beliefs, which are not truly yours until you examine them and decide whether you want to keep them, is that you will be able to sift through them and let go of those beliefs that are not helping you learn and grow.

Affirmation: As I look at my past relationships, I let go of blame and look within myself to determine what I can learn that will help me in my self-growth journey.

43. If it really takes one to tango, you can do wonders for your marriage.

Maybe you don't believe that you can make a difference in your marriage all by yourself. Maybe you feel like you don't **want** to make the effort to help your marriage unless your spouse is onboard with you. Maybe you believe that you've tried everything to help your marriage and nothing has worked.

I've witnessed some amazing changes in my clients who have said that regardless of what their spouse did or didn't do, they were committed to helping their relationship. It does make a difference. I've also seen plenty of clients who remained stuck because they refused to budge unless they saw their spouse start making changes first. They remained locked in a score-keeping power struggle.

One of my clients came to see me about how she could deal with her alcoholic husband. She said she was a strong believer in the sanctity of marriage and that because of her religious beliefs, she did not believe in divorce except in extreme cases such as physical violence.

She asked me to help her learn to live more joyfully within her marriage. She had seen previous therapists who had encouraged her to leave her husband. She told me in no uncertain terms how she felt about therapists trying to get her to do what she did not want to do. Believe me, I heard her loud and clear and I paid attention!

I worked with her individually and never even laid eyes on her husband. Over the time we worked together, we focused on her behavior. She admitted that this was her typical pattern with her husband: the more he drank the more she nagged him, trying to stop him from drinking as much as he did. We looked at how ineffective this strategy was and together we developed a plan for her.

She decided to stop nagging. This may seem simplistic, but she noticed that when she greeted him warmly when he arrived home each day and said nothing at all when he began to drink, he actually engaged her in pleasant conversation and ended up drinking less.

The simplest solution is often to do more of what works and less of what does not. In this woman's case, we found that when she was willing to shift her behavior, even a little, she got more of what she wanted, which was conversation and a feeling of closeness with her husband. He did not stop drinking altogether, but that was not the reason she came to see me.

She was not going to stop him from drinking. That was his behavior to work on, not hers. When she accepted this and chose to focus on herself and the behaviors she **could** change that she was doing, she was able to affect her relationship with her husband in a positive way.

Action step:

Ask yourself the following Choice Theory question and make a commitment to doing whatever you think will help your marriage.

- ☐ What am I willing to do on a regular and consistent basis, regardless of what my spouse does or does not do, that I think will help my marriage? Important: begin with small steps.
- ☐ Write your answer in your journal.
- ☐ Decide when you will begin this new behavior and keep track of how often you succeed in doing what you are committing to do.
- ☐ Notice any changes in your interaction with your spouse.

Be patient. Remember, this isn't McDonalds! Most changes don't happen instantly, though you may be pleasantly surprised at how soon you notice some changes for the better.

Affirmation: I am committed to doing what I can do that will help my relationship. I can do more than I think I can.

44. When you let go of the need to "fix" your spouse, you can concentrate on your personal growth.

I'm a work in progress, as are most of my fellow human beings. I still have a lot of work to do on myself and I welcome the opportunity to focus on my life-long task of self growth. I have so much to do to improve myself that I have no time to spare to focus on fixing my husband. Can you relate?

As a recovering Control Freak, I can relate to my clients who complain about back seat driving. I was the worst! I listen to "Car Talk" on National Public Radio as often as I can. I remember during one of the shows, Tom and Ray were discussing the difference between men and women drivers. One of them (I don't remember if it was Tom or Ray) said that when he gets into the car he plans out his entire route in his head and then he starts driving.

He said his wife gets into the car and always leaves the house in the same way, regardless of her destination. For example, she would always go left out of the driveway. I laughed, because I was the one who had a mental map of my destination and a plan for where I was going. My late husband Al would drive like the wife!

I'm not proud to admit that I felt it was my job to correct him. I did get better at controlling myself instead of trying to fix him, yet it took years for me to just be a passenger and enjoy the ride with my husband.

Action step:

In letting go of the need to fix your spouse, you will come up against a lot of resistance. This resistance to change your bad habits is normal. No one wants to give up control. Believe me, I know. I didn't either, even though I knew it would help my marriage.

- ☐ Pick one thing you are doing to try to fix your spouse that you know is causing friction.
- ☐ Make a conscious decision to reduce and eventually eliminate that behavior.

- ☐ Using the back seat driving example, decide to simply enjoy the ride without saying anything. You could use the time to enjoy conversing or listening to music or an audio book.
- ☐ Tell yourself, "We'll get there when we get there" if you think your spouse drives too slowly, takes too many "short cuts," or uses highly congested routes out of habit.
- ☐ Close your eyes if you notice that your spouse is not breaking as soon as you would. It's amazing how that allows you to calm yourself when you cannot see!
- ☐ Trust your spouse to get you there safely, especially if s/he has a safe driving history.
- ☐ Remember: it's all small stuff.
- ☐ If your spouse is doing something that you react to with fear, it's all right to request a behavior change. Remember: make a request, not a demand.

Affirmation: I am concentrating on my personal growth. I let go of the need to fix my spouse.

45. If you believe you are responsible for co-creating a successful marriage, do all you can to make it happen.

Yes, you are responsible for co-creating your happy, successful marriage. Now what? Knowing something is a first step. It's easy to get bogged down in the details. It's also easy to start feeling responsible for making everything perfect. Realize that every step you take toward creating your happy marriage, even a tiny one, is progress.

If you are going to do it well, let go of the need for your spouse to be on the same program at the same time. Your spouse's job is to participate willingly in her/his own self-growth journey at a pace that works for her/him, not you. You both work on your contribution to your happy, healthy relationship beginning by focusing on your own self-improvement.

Action step:

Here are some quick and easy steps to take toward your goal of creating your successful marriage:

- ☐ Daily doses of appreciation go a long way toward creating feelings of goodwill.
- ☐ Focus on what is going right, notice it, and thank your spouse. Adults need to hear that they are doing a good job just as much as children do.
- ☐ Smiles, hugs, and kisses are quick and easy and usually welcome. So are quick notes of praise and appreciation posted in surprising places.
- ☐ Let go of perfection. Your way to fold laundry may not be your spouse's way, but who cares? It's one less thing on your "to do" list and the job got done, right?

Affirmation: I am a co-creator in my happy, successful marriage.

46. Successful couples take personal responsibility for their thoughts and interpretations.

You bring your relationship history into every argument you have with your spouse. The way you interpret how your spouse behaves has everything to do with your own history and often little to do with your spouse, although you may have married someone who has similar patterns to those you are familiar with.

It's still boils down to the meaning you give to the situation. This is what causes you pain, not your spouse's behavior. This may be a hard pill to swallow, especially if you have been accustomed to blaming external events and other people for your unhappiness.

Action step:

Name an event about which you had some strong, negative feelings. Record your thoughts and feelings in your journal completing the following sentences:

- ☐ When it happened I felt _____.
- ☐ This is what I made it mean _____.
- ☐ This is how I acted as a result of my thoughts about this event _____.
- ☐ This is how I treated my spouse as a result of my interpretation of this event _____.
- ☐ This is what I want to do with the information I have discovered about myself _____.

Be patient and forgiving as you do this exercise. You may discover some things about yourself and your behavior that may disturb you. These are behaviors, beliefs, and attitudes you have been hiding from yourself.

You may realize that you have been quite harsh and judging. You may even discover you are not as nice as you have believed yourself to be. Before you start condemning yourself, realize this: self-discovery gives you an opportunity. That opportunity is for you to do something new, and something more loving, including forgiving yourself.

Be careful to avoid getting bogged down in black and white, all or nothing thinking. Relationships come in all sorts of shades of gray. If you insist things must be this way or that, you will most likely find yourself in constant conflict. Let flexibility be your guide.

Affirmation: What I say and do has more to do with me and my personal history than about what my spouse has said or done. The same is true for my spouse.

47. If you do not take care of yourself first, you will be in poor shape to take care of anyone else.

Put the oxygen mask on your own face first. You cannot help anyone if you are unconscious!

I love hearing the flight attendant reminding us that "in the unlikely event of loss of cabin pressure, oxygen masks will be deployed. Place the mask on your own face first...then assist others." What they don't say is that it takes less than 60 seconds for you to become unconscious and then (soon after) die from lack of oxygen, so it is critical that you take care of yourself first before you attend to others.

My sister Kimberly runs half marathons several times a year. She has found that running is something she enjoys and that she actually needs to run to feel good physically. Is that selfish? Of course not. When she takes care of herself, she is in a better position to be present for her husband and children.

I encourage you to do something each day for yourself. A little "me" time allows you to be able to feel good about yourself and to return to your spouse and family refreshed and more able to give your time and energy to those you love.

How can you apply this lesson in your every day life?

Action step:

- ☐ Do one thing every day that is just for you: take a walk, read a book, take a bubble bath, work on a hobby, or do something totally frivolous.
- ☐ Allow yourself to take time for you, knowing you will be refreshed and able to give your love, time, and energy to your loved ones as a result.

Affirmation: I am worthy of taking care of myself. I take care of myself happily and my loved ones benefit as a result.

48. Drop your anger shield and allow love to enter your life.

Anger often masks fear. If you can step back in the face someone's anger and see the fear behind it, you can find your compassion.

I do not claim for an instant that it is easy to remain calm when someone you love is expressing some heavy duty anger. It takes a lot of determination and practice to stand calmly through someone else's storm.

So many people have loved and lost. The feelings of hurt, sadness, and anger are almost universal. You can probably relate to the pain of a relationship that ended badly. Maybe you have experienced this pain repeatedly. If you're someone who has loved and lost more than once, you may have developed a hard outer shell, like a Shield of Anger. Now, when you think of loving again, you may feel cynical, not hopeful and expectant.

The problem with holding onto this anger is that you still want a relationship. You still yearn to be connected to someone special, but you doubt it's possible. You may think that love is not going to come to you and you are doomed to remain alone or in a bad relationship.

Anger serves an important function for you. It protects you from more hurt. If you walk around with anger oozing from every pore, people avoid you. No one can hurt you if they cannot get near enough. Unfortunately, keeping people at arm's length keeps you isolated. Like most humans, you are a social creature and you want to be connected. But it's too scary and painful to let go of the anger that protects you.

Action step:

- ☐ Acknowledge the hurt of the lost relationship. Pretending you are "just fine" keeps you stuck.
- ☐ Look at how you contributed to the problems in the broken relationship. It's called a "relationship" because two people are involved. Don't take on the entire blame, but rather accept your responsibility for your part.
- ☐ Notice the patterns that you keep repeating in your relationships. What is the same in each one? What negative traits are common? What red flags do you keep ignoring?
- ☐ Keep your observations in your journal as you notice these patterns.
- ☐ Learn all you can about creating new patterns. Read, hire a coach, join a support group, talk to trustworthy friends and family, and so on.

Affirmation: I now let go of the Shield of Anger so that I can connect more fully with those I love.

49. Decide what is so important that you absolutely have to keep it. The rest is negotiable.

Benjamin and his wife, Sharon came to see me because of constant arguments. As I learned more about the way they related to each other, I noticed a pattern that was evident, even in the short time we interacted. When Benjamin and Sharon would tell me about their latest conflict, Benjamin explained, "That's the way we did it in my family," as if that was all that needed to be said.

I realized that this couple was engaged in a power struggle and "that's the way we did it in my family" was Benjamin's battle cry. He would use this statement to explain and later to justify why they "should" do things his way. He was not aware or interested in learning that there were many ways to do things that differed from his family's particular way. Sharon was frustrated and fed up with her husband's rally cry, but she didn't know what else to do but argue. She felt she was being punished for having a different way of doing things.

Some traditions are important to you. So important that you would mourn their loss. Others are negotiable. Decide which traditions are so important that you cannot let them go.

The problem this couple had was that Benjamin could not distinguish between important and trivial traditions. How you fold socks and how you wash dishes are not earth shattering traditions. I'm amazed, though, at how vehemently some couples argue about the "correct" way to do every day household chores.

If you use "the way we did it" for everything from the right way to celebrate holidays to the correct application of the toilet paper onto the holder, you are setting your marriage up for continual strife. What is this really about? Control. It says, "I want my life to be an exact reflection of my childhood and I want my spouse to jump on board and get with the program. **My Program.**"

It also says that you are unwilling to examine other possibilities. Your family did not have the corner on the only right way to do things. So if you are interested in opening your mind to new ways of being and doing, consider having a talk with your spouse. Begin by listing three things that are most important to you. These would be things you feel so strongly about that you would be hard-pressed to give up doing them your particular way.

Instead of using the tired old argument of "that's the way we did it in my family," focus on explaining what makes that particular way of doing things important to you. Make sure you tell your spouse that you understand it's not the only way to do it, but that for you, it's very important.

Next, list some things that you have insisted on doing a particular way that you can let go of. **If you're having a hard time letting go of anything, you need to work on why this is so before you can let it go.**

For example, if you and your spouse take turns doing the dishes and you've been hovering over your spouse's shoulder to make sure the chore is done the "right" way, agree to stay out of the kitchen when it's not your turn. Or, if you are unwilling to do that, agree that you will always be the one to do the dishes.

These kinds of power struggles suck the positive energy out of a relationship. Is it worth it? If you answered "no" then good for you. You realize that your marriage is more important than doing it your way. If you insist on stubbornly holding on to a "my way or the highway" attitude, you may find yourself alone. Your marriage is an evolving, living, breathing entity. If you choose to create a dictatorship, it may work in the short run if you have a willing doormat for a spouse. However, even the most easy-going people have their limits.

Action step:

Decide which traditions are worth holding onto. Write these things in your journal. Often, bigger things like religious celebrations, how you like to spend your vacations and holidays, and how you manage money will show up on your list. Even big traditions can be negotiated to allow both spouses to be satisfied.

Next ask yourself these questions about your traditions:

- ☐ What makes this tradition important to me?
- ☐ How can I be flexible about this tradition?
- ☐ If I'm not willing to be flexible, what is the likely outcome?
- ☐ Am I willing to accept that my spouse does things differently than I do and to decide that it's perfectly all right?

Affirmation: I am flexible. I let go of the need to do things my way. I accept that there are plenty of other acceptable ways to do things.

50. Conflict, while uncomfortable, can teach you so much about yourself.

Most people become uncomfortable when they are in conflict with others. This is a good thing. If you were at ease and enjoyed arguing, you might do it all the time! You might even find reasons to prolong conflict, or start problems with those you love just for the thrill of it.

Some people live on the extremes of the bell curve, some avoiding conflict at all costs, others seeking and instigating conflicts like verbal daredevils. Most people are happy to remain in the center of the curve, and I suspect you are one of those people. If you would like to learn more about yourself, how you manage yourself during conflicts is a good place to start. Once you do this exercise, usually after a conflict, you will learn some things that you can use to guide you during your next conflict.

"But I don't like conflicts," you say. Of course you don't. The thing is, conflicts are a part of life. You cannot avoid all of them, so it's best to gain some insight and learn how to address them when they do happen.

Here is an example of what might happen during a conflict:

Joe looks at Sandy with what she interprets as an angry expression. Sandy feels an immediate reaction in her stomach. She feels like she's going to be sick. Joe says he cannot find his keys. Irrationally, Sandy feels guilty and leaps up to start helping him look for the keys, even though she doesn't drive his car and is not responsible for his set of keys.

Sandy starts to feel resentful, thinking, "Why can't he keep up with his keys? Why should I have to help him?" She wants to leave the house, leaving him to his search. She judges him as being unorganized. Sandy keeps her thoughts to herself, though, because the last time she told him what was on her mind, they yelled at each other and then gave each other the cold shoulder for the next three days.

There is a lot of useful information for Sandy here:

- ☐ She interprets Joe's frustration as anger and feels it directed toward her, regardless of whether that is true.
- ☐ She feels physically ill.
- ☐ The feeling in her stomach probably comes from fear.
- ☐ She feels resentment and anger toward Joe, even if he didn't "cause" her feelings.
- ☐ She wants to flee, but instead stays to help, thinking that she "should" help.
- ☐ She remembers that last time she spoke her mind, she and Joe argued, so she holds in her resentment to avoid further conflict. This is an example of fleeing rather than fighting.

Where did this come from? On the surface it looks like Sandy's reaction is over the top. If we were to examine things in greater detail, we would discover that Sandy grew up in a house where Daddy raged whenever he got frustrated. Sandy watched as her mother did all she could to placate her father. This observation taught her that an angry man must be appeased.

Fortunately, your childhood does not have to dictate your adulthood. You can learn new skills and apply them when certain behaviors trigger old childhood programming. The first step is to acknowledge the origins of your reactions and begin to unlink the chains that are binding you so that you can learn new skills. Once you replace old reactions with new skills, you will create new, more positive links to replace the old chains of childhood.

Action step:

Think about the last conflict you were involved in with your spouse (or anyone you care about). Write the answers to the following questions with as much detail as you can:

- ☐ What was going on at the time?
- ☐ A lot of people experience certain physiological reactions to stressful situations. What did you notice was going on in your body? Where was the tension?
- ☐ How were you feeling emotionally?
- ☐ The Lizard Brain may kick in, giving you a desire to Fight, Flee, or Freeze. What were you thinking about doing at the time?
- ☐ Your thoughts influence your feelings. You cannot feel without a thought. What automatic thoughts came up for you during the conflict?

Sandy can help herself by talking to herself in a new way. She could say, "My body is reacting to old programming. Joe is not doing anything **to** me. I can help him find his keys, but he is not demanding that I do so."

When she does her "self talk" in this way, she is able to calm herself and stop the downhill slide toward feeling angry, resentful, and fearful, which are her old programs creeping into her current relationship. She can now choose how she will feel as she begins to think differently.

Affirmation: The more I understand myself, the more I am able to let go of the behaviors that no longer serve me. I understand that conflict is a normal part of life. I am developing new skills to deal with conflict more effectively.

Self-Control:

When "That's Just the Way I Am" Won't Cut it Anymore

"You cannot control what happens to you, but you can control your attitude toward what happens to you, and in that, you will be mastering change rather than allowing it to master you." Brian Tracy

51. Exercising self-control is a cornerstone of a happy, successful relationship.

I think that self-control is something many people would be wise to exercise but few master. Failing to exercise self-control, people turn to controlling others as a way to deal with feeling out of control.

That's where the Seven Deadly Habits come into play. When people are unhappy, especially in intimate relationships, they turn to the one they love and (sadly) decide that their unhappiness is coming from outside themselves.

They point a finger at their spouse and exclaim, "You're supposed to make me happy!" Then they proceed to criticize, blame, complain, nag, threaten, punish, and reward/bribe to get their spouse to do something about their unhappiness. All along, the happiness (and unhappiness) comes from within. Instead of working on themselves, they look outside of themselves for that elusive happiness.

The unhappiness is coming from the story they are telling themselves about the situation at hand (any situation will do). Self-control does take a lot of practice. It means focusing on what you have determined to do, how you have decided to act, regardless of what someone else is doing (or not doing).

Many of my clients are professionals who have learned highly effective communication skills in their work to deal with people who are unhappy, angry, or downright mean and nasty. They are quite skilled in helping irate, irritable people transform into satisfied customers. My clients are great problem-solvers and creative thinkers!

Once most people leave their place of employment, they take off their "work hat" and put on their "home hat." For the most part, this is a very good thing. Taking your work home can lead to stress at home. What I propose is a bit different. I ask my clients to leave work at work, but to take home the helpful communication skills. This doesn't mean that if you are an attorney you put your spouse on trial or if you are a doctor you diagnose your spouse.

When I ask my clients how they deal with difficult people in their jobs, they often say things like:

- ☐ I usually let them vent for a while.
- ☐ I express sympathy.
- ☐ I look at the situations from their side.
- ☐ I make sure they feel understood.
- ☐ I listen before I try to solve anything.
- ☐ I ask, "What can I do to help?"
- ☐ I maintain self-control.
- ☐ I don't take what they say personally.

After I tell my clients that I'm impressed with their skills (and I truly am) I ask them which of these skills they can take home with them. Sometimes they are astonished that they have the skills; they often see it as "just part of the job" and don't appreciate that they have some pretty amazing abilities.

Now, bringing home these skills is a bit tricky. Usually you are not emotionally invested in the outcome with a difficult client or customer. With your spouse, it's harder to remain logical and your emotions do come into play, sometimes quite strongly.

Sometimes this results in normally mature, self-controlled adults regressing into children fighting in the schoolyard. The same emotional connection that allows you to express loving thoughts to each other is the one that gives you the idea that it's all right to yell at each other and say harmful things to each other.

Action step:

- ☐ List all of your work-related people skills in your journal.
- ☐ Give yourself a big pat on the back! I'll wait…
- ☐ Ask yourself which of these skills you can put to use immediately in your relationship.

Answer these questions carefully and write your responses in your journal:

- ☐ As you work on self-control what are you telling yourself about the situation at hand that keeps you going back to your default behavior?
- ☐ Are you allowing someone else's behavior (like your spouse, for instance) to determine how you will act?

Affirmation: I understand the value of self-control and I strive to exercise self-control daily, especially in my relationship with the one I love.

52. Self-improvement is a wonderful endeavor. "Fixing" others is not.

As I teach my clients new skills, I often chuckle quietly as I notice that they continue the old patterns along with the new skills. I teach all my clients about the basics of Choice Theory and I always recommend that they read any of the books Dr. William Glasser has written in the last ten years.

Here's an example. I tell my clients about the Seven Deadly Habits of External Control. I then ask them to identify their habit of choice, which is the one they tend to use most often. I ask them to decide what they will do differently between now and the next time we meet.

Often when I see them again they tell me they recognized the Deadly Habits in their spouse. Their next step was to tell their spouse, "You're using a Deadly Habit." I laugh because I did the same things my clients were doing when I was first learning Choice Theory.

So, while they are learning something beneficial, they are still holding onto external control. Now they are pointing out the Deadly Habits to each other. It makes sense. People still return to their default behavior even when they are learning new skills and habits.

Action step:

- ☐ As you work on your own self-improvement, it is natural for you to want your spouse to improve also. Notice when you are focused on your spouse and gently remind yourself that your job is to take care of your own self-growth, not your spouse's.

Affirmation: I notice when I am tempted to fix my spouse and I gently refocus on my own self-growth.

53. Even though you're married you still need to mind your manners.

Where have all the manners gone? I'm amazed at how being polite seems to be a vanishing art. Recently, I've seen articles online about how Americans are less well-mannered than in previous years. Taken as a whole, if Americans are less polite, this is affecting every area of society. Where I see it doing the most damage is in intimate relationships.

Maybe you would never do this. Or maybe you can relate:

When you first met your future spouse, you put on your "dating face." You showed your best side and minded your manners. After all, you wanted to make a good impression.

As you got to know each other, you began to get comfortable. Sometimes too comfortable! You may have begun to "let it all hang out." Maybe you started showing your sloppy habits or even began acting in a way that could be obnoxious. You began to expect your chosen one to accept you as you were.

Once you developed a committed relationship, you may have even stopped minding your manners at all, and then blamed your spouse when s/he called you on the carpet, saying, "You knew I was this way when you met me."

When people choose to marry, they say they will cherish each other. They promise to love and respect each other. They agree to hold their partnership as valuable. Yet, soon after (or maybe even before they marry) they begin to treat their partners with contempt, disrespect, and sometimes even with cruelty. Sometimes they even treat strangers better than the one they chose to love.

Is that just the way it is? Not necessarily, but it can be. It's understandable that you will relax as you become comfortable with another person. It doesn't mean you have to relax your manners. I don't mean being stiff and formal with your spouse. But it's important to keep up the good habits that you used to win your spouse's heart.

Nothing is "just the way it is" that you didn't choose to make that way. To say, "That's just the way I am" is the same as admitting that you refuse to accept responsibility for your behavior. When you treat your spouse with contempt, you are acting contemptibly. When you disrespect your partner, you are disrespecting yourself and your relationship.

Let's play "Remember When."

Sometimes in the course of everyday life, with the stresses of work, children, household chores, and social obligations, you may be hard-pressed to remember why you married your spouse. It's a good idea to play the reminiscing game on a regular basis to remind yourselves why you made a commitment to each other.

It's also important that you remember to be playful with this exercise. This is not meant to be yet another chore. Remembering the great times can bring a smile to your face. When you smile and laugh with each other you reduce those stressful feelings and your brain releases all sorts of wonderful feel-good hormones.

Action step:

Play "Remember When" with these questions to start you off:

- ☐ When you first met and began dating each other, how did you interact?
- ☐ What attracted you to your spouse back then?
- ☐ What was your favorite activity?
- ☐ What do you remember fondly about those days?
- ☐ What were some things that endeared you to your spouse when you first met?

Now, bring this exercise home. Think about your behavior toward your spouse when the two of you were first getting to know each other. These may be things you are still doing or they may be long-forgotten courtesies that you can reestablish in your treatment of each other.

- ☐ How did you treat each other when you were first getting to know each other?
- ☐ What things did you do to endear yourself to each other?
- ☐ When you wanted to express something uncomfortable, what did you do that may be different now?
- ☐ How did you handle disagreements?
- ☐ What annoying behaviors did you laugh off, thinking, "It's no big deal?" (small things, not large, deal-breaking behaviors)
- ☐ Did you give your future spouse a break over minor things back when you were dating? Are you still doing that now?

Finally, it's time to bring the things that worked well in the past back into the present. If it worked before, chances are it can work again.

- ☐ What have you stopped doing that was helpful?
- ☐ What can you start doing again that will bring back the respect and loving feelings to your relationship?
- ☐ What helpful behaviors would you like to bring back into your relationship that you think will bring the two of you closer?

Affirmation: I remember when I met my spouse fondly and I focus on maintaining the good manners that helped us fall in love with each other.

54. "Judge not that ye be not judged" is a good rule for marriage.

Some people are recovering alcoholics; I'm someone who is recovering from being judgmental. Yes, I spent much of my childhood and early adulthood judging others and feeling a sense of superiority over them because I knew better and I was on the right path. The older I get the less I feel the need to be judgmental, but I admit it's not all gone!

In my early days as a therapist, I worked for the Family Violence Prevention Services in San Antonio, Texas. I had the privilege to have as my supervisor the late Eugene Brown, who once told me a parable that was meant especially for me. I was in my late 20's and I didn't understand it until years later:

It went something like this:

> A young man, full of ambition and a desire to help others, prayed that he would be given the ability to change the world. Years went by and he was not as successful at changing the world as he had hoped.
>
> As he became a mature, middle-aged man, he was tired, but he still wanted to help, so he prayed for the ability to change his community. He was a bit more successful in this task, but again not as successful as he would have liked.
>
> As an elderly man he finally figured it out. He prayed simply for the ability to change himself.

It took him all his life to realize that the only person he could change was himself. I had similar aspirations to the man in this story, but my problem was that I believed that if people would just do things my way (which in my judgment was the only right way to do things) life would be so much easier for them and more importantly, for me.

I have been blessed to discover this elusive truth earlier in my life though I still struggle with it. And yes, it affected how I treated Al since I believed I was right and he "should" do things my way.

Action step:

- ☐ If you are more focused on your spouse's faults than you are your own, let go of this. You have enough to do to improve your own behavior.
- ☐ When you fall back into the default behavior of judging, don't judge yourself harshly when you recognize it. Just notice it and gently move yourself toward kinder, more loving thoughts.
- ☐ Recognize that new habits take some time to become part of the new you.

Affirmation: I let go of judging my spouse. I also let go of judging myself for holding judgments against my spouse.

55. I feel bad so I get to treat you badly? In which universe, exactly, is this okay?

Whenever you think you cannot change your feelings, remember this quote by the very first First Lady, Martha Washington:

"I am determined to be cheerful and happy in whatever situation I may find myself. For I have learned that the greater part of our misery or unhappiness is determined not by our circumstance but by our disposition."

Although I was born several decades afterward, I absolutely adore the Big Band era. I began listening to this wonderful music of the 1930's and 1940's as a child. One of my favorite groups of this era is the Mills Brothers. One of their songs puzzled me when I was a child, though. Here is a portion of the lyrics for the song, "You Always Hurt the One You Love":

> You always hurt the one you love
> The one you shouldn't hurt at all...
> So if I broke your heart last night
> It's because I love you most of all.

It is true that people often treat the ones they are closest to with the greatest disrespect, contempt, and lack of positive regard. Where did the idea come from that just because you are married you have the right to treat your spouse badly? Like many things learned in childhood, this is yet another one. People learn through observation, maybe not at home, but through the culture they grow up in, through the media, through school, or other means.

"I'm having a bad day" is something you tell yourself when things are not going the way you had hoped or planned. You feel frustrated and impatient, unhappy with the way things are. You have interpreted this as meaning you are having a bad day. You may even decide that things will continue to "go wrong" for the rest of the day.

Sometimes when people decide that they are unhappy and irritable, they excuse themselves from exercising self-control. They snap at their loved ones, thinking, "I'm having a bad day." They spread their "bad day" virus to others, who, in turn, infect even more people.

Some people treat everyone badly when they are "having a bad day." Others reserve their grouchy behavior for those they love the most. **If you notice that you are treating strangers with more kindness than your loved ones, it becomes quite obvious that you are choosing your behavior.** You can choose to turn this around.

Action step:

- ☐ Do some self-calming practices, whatever works for you: slow and deep breathing, prayer, Yoga, exercise, meditation, listening to music, visiting your favorite place in nature, taking a mental vacation, petting your cat/dog, listening to soothing music, drinking a **mental** margarita, and so on.
- ☐ Decide now to refuse to allow the notion of a "bad day" into your mind. The day is what it is. Ask yourself instead, "Why has this happened *for* me?
- ☐ Ask for help and understanding when you need it. Share your frustrations. People can be amazingly understanding when you include them and ask for help and understanding.
- ☐ Decide that despite your difficulties, you are going to see them as learning opportunities. Treat the people around you kindly. Notice their response to you. Often this can lift your spirits, since people generally respond to kindness with more of the same.
- ☐ Your feelings are related to what you are thinking. Find something about your situation to be grateful for. Focus on this. When you stop focusing on "how bad things are" and focus instead on what you can learn and what you are appreciate, your feelings start to change.

Affirmation: I choose to see difficult situations as learning opportunities. I treat the ones I love with kindness even when I am dealing with difficulties.

> **56. When you are committed to your own self-growth, it gets easier to let go of the need to fix others.**

As a recovering Control Freak I am going to tell on myself. For a very long time it was important to me that my late husband Al do things my way. I would ask him to help me in the kitchen and he would willingly cut up all sorts of vegetables while I prepared a meal. My problem was that instead of appreciating his help, I criticized his way of cutting veggies!

I wanted the asparagus in one inch slices and he cut them into half inch slices. I wanted the onions minced very fine and he only chopped them coarsely. Part of the problem was that I didn't make myself clear about what I wanted. Another problem was that I expected him to read my mind and automatically know exactly how I wanted it.

The biggest problem was that I didn't bother to ask myself these questions, which I ask myself now:

- ☐ Why is it so important that he do it my way?
- ☐ Who says he has to do anything the way I want it done?

He was doing me a favor. I didn't "need" his help; I wanted his company. When Al and I attended Dr. Glasser's day-long workshop on Choice Theory, I began to understand just how controlling I was being. I cannot say that I mended my Control Freak ways in a day or a month or even a year, but that workshop was the beginning of a change for the better for me.

As I let go of the need to control Al, I noticed that he was more relaxed around me. I would often tell people that Choice Theory saved my marriage. If Al, ever my gracious husband, was present when I told them that, he would always say, "Our marriage was great and it still is," or something along those lines.

The truth for me is that Choice Theory helped me to stop using the Seven Deadly Habits as frequently, and to eventually get rid of those unhelpful behaviors that created tension in my marriage. It made me aware that I had a choice to continue trying to fix my husband (who was not broken) or work on improving my own behavior toward him.

As I began to let go of my need to control, when I asked for Al's help and he did it, I expressed appreciation for the gift he gave me. That was definitely progress for me.

Action step:

If you are using the Seven Deadly Habits in your everyday interactions with your spouse, now is the time to do some serious self-reflecting. Ask yourself the questions I asked myself earlier in this section. Add to them this all-important question:

☐ How important is my marriage to me?

Is your marriage more important than your need to have things done your way? I sincerely hope so!

Affirmation: My self-growth journey is all about me. I am willing to invest time, effort, and energy to become the best I can be.

57. Words can soothe or they can be terrible weapons.

You are powerful. Your words have power. The people you love, especially your spouse, are affected by your words, for good or ill. Knowing that you have this incredible power, how will you use it?

Sometimes people excuse themselves by saying, "It just slipped out" or "I wasn't thinking" or even "I didn't mean it." The brain processes thoughts a lot faster than you can speak. The words you say are thoughts in your brain before they come out of your mouth. So no more excuses!

Action step:

> If you have a habit of blurting things out before you think about the consequences of your words, you can change this if you're willing. You'll feel even more powerful when you exercise self-control. Here are some ideas to get you started:
>
> ☐ Think about the last time you said something that created discomfort or even pain. Ask yourself what else you could say that would be more helpful.
> ☐ If you are scratching your head right now, ask someone you trust to give you honest feedback (not to just say, "Oh, no, you're fine.").

Affirmation: I examine my words and consider the impact they could have on others before I speak them.

> **58. Just as in carpentry, "measure twice, cut once" works well when speaking. Measure your words twice before you speak.**

My Dad takes the time to compose what he will say before he says it. Other family members used to poke fun at this behavior, saying things like, "I'm going to take a nap while you decide what your answer is." I think my Dad has a good thing going. It used to annoy me when I was in a hurry and wanted a quick response. Now I respect it and I emulate him as often as I can remember to do so.

When my Dad was in his teens, he worked with my maternal grandfather (my Mom's father), who was a carpenter. I've never asked him, but I wonder if this lesson of measuring twice had any impact on the way my father became so careful about measuring his words. Measuring twice before cutting boards is a smart thing to do. So is measuring the impact of your words before they leave your mouth.

Too often when you rush to defend yourself you say things that are not helpful. What do you imagine will happen when you slow down and think about what you want to say before you say it? Experiment and find out for yourself.

Action step:

- ☐ Take this lesson from the field of carpentry: measure your words twice and measure carefully before you decide to say them.
- ☐ When you have something especially difficult to say, take some time to write your thoughts out. It's all right if you want to read what you have written to your spouse once you are finished composing it.

Affirmation: I now take the time to choose my words carefully, thinking about how they may affect my loved ones before I speak them aloud.

59. A closed mouth gathers no foot.

Moms everywhere have often said, "If you don't have something nice to say, say nothing at all." This is sage advice from one of our first teachers. Do you remember to apply this advice to the ones you love most of all? Often people are kinder to strangers than to their loved ones. This is most likely because of the familiarity factor. You are comfortable with your loved ones and feel free to express yourself in loving **and** not so loving ways.

Once the words are out there, they linger. Sometimes they can even poison the relationship. If you are constantly putting your foot in your mouth, you might want to consider your words carefully before you say them. Avoid "foot in mouth disease" by practicing monitoring your thoughts.

Action step:

- ☐ Ask yourself whether it is necessary for you to say what you are thinking.
- ☐ Ask yourself how your spouse is likely to respond to your words.
- ☐ Ask yourself whether there is another way to express what is on your mind that is more likely to be received favorably.

Affirmation: I pause before I speak, examining my thoughts to make sure my message is helpful and clear.

60. Just because you think it doesn't mean you must speak it.

Sometimes people believe that they must say whatever comes to their minds. They may not want to stifle themselves or maybe they have never been taught about discretion and tact. Some people believe they must be totally honest. Sadly, one person's idea of honesty is another person's opinion. Sometimes your private thoughts are best kept to yourself, especially if they will hurt the ones you love.

The movie "The Invention of Lying" is about a society where people say exactly what is on their minds without any regard for the feelings of the person receiving the message. They tell the "absolute truth" as they see it. The people have no filtering system. They seem to be incapable of remaining silent if a thought comes to their minds, so they say things like, "I'm intimidated by you" or "You'll always be a loser."

When you speak remember this acrostic for tact:

TACT: Talk **A**fter **C**areful **T**hought

Action step:

- ☐ Think before speaking and remember to use tact.
- ☐ Determine to monitor your thoughts. Pause before you decide to say something that could possibly help you feel better for a moment, but cause pain to you and the one you love.

Affirmation: I monitor my thoughts and speak carefully.

61. Do you believe in total honesty? What if what you want to say is not helpful? Or just an opinion?

Sometimes people confuse their opinion with honesty. As I said earlier in this book, just because you believe something doesn't mean it is helpful or "the truth." Some people may even say harmful or cruel things and excuse their behavior by following up with, "I'm just being honest." They may even recruit others to defend their "honest" words by saying, "I'm just saying what others are thinking" or worse, "I'm the only one here who is honest enough to say it."

Action step:

Do you recognize yourself in the above paragraph? If so, here are some ideas for you:

- ☐ When you are about to share something with your spouse, pause. Ask yourself, "Is what I'm about to say going to help or hurt?"
- ☐ Examine your thoughts and ask if what you think is really "just being honest" or an opinion. Remember: just because you believe it doesn't make it true.
- ☐ Decide whether what you are about to say is important enough to risk hurting your spouse. If you think it is, be careful about how you send your message. Spend some time thinking about what you want to say, even composing it on paper before presenting your thoughts to your spouse.

Do you know others who do this?

- ☐ Retaliation usually makes things worse, so be polite.
- ☐ If you have experienced hurtful comments in the guise of "honesty," recognize them for what they are, thank the person for sharing, saying something like, "Thanks for letting me know what's on your mind." Then change the subject or excuse yourself from the situation.

Affirmation: I know the value of examining my thoughts and I am careful to distinguish between my opinion and honesty.

62. Most stuff is small stuff. Don't make mountains out of molehills.

"Don't sweat the small stuff...and it's all small stuff." Richard Carlson

Recently I read an article online about the top ten things couples argue about. This article claimed that couples argue an average of 312 times a year. I was astonished, given that there are only 365 days in a year. The things the couples were arguing about most frequently, according to the article, were levels of cleanliness in the bathroom and kitchen.

Can you relate? Do you and your spouse argue about small stuff? Do you complain about the right way to load the dishwasher or get wrapped around the axle about the toothpaste being squeezed in the middle?

If so, you are wasting your time on trivialities. Life is so short and getting upset about the small stuff takes away from your quality of life. I would prefer to see you enjoying your life with your spouse rather than spinning your wheels carping about the small stuff.

Action step:

This is not to say that you cannot ask for change. Asking is not the same as nagging unless you keep repeating yourself. Just be sure you do it in a loving way and realize that just because you ask for it doesn't mean your spouse is going to be willing or able to give you what you want.

- ☐ Ask your spouse if this is a good time to talk. If you get a positive response, proceed. If not, ask to schedule a brief time together, suggesting later in the evening or the next day.
- ☐ When you do talk, keep it short and to the point.
- ☐ Thank your spouse honoring your request to sit and talk with you.
- ☐ You may start with something you do appreciate about your spouse, and own the fact that you are uncomfortable about a certain behavior you want to address. Own your own craziness!

Things that bother you may not bother your spouse at all and that is okay.

- [ ] No hitting below the belt. It's NOT all right to say, "You are such a slob! Why did I ever marry you?"
- [ ] Remember Joe Friday on "Dragnet" and his famous line of "Just the facts, ma-am"? No finger pointing. Ask for the change that you want. No demands; this is a request. It's all right to say, "I notice you leave your dirty socks all over the bedroom floor (fact). I would really appreciate your putting them in the hamper when you are done wearing them (request)."
- [ ] If your spouse decides to play tit for tat, be careful not to be drawn into it. If the two of you have been in the habit of blaming each other, it's likely that when you first do this your spouse will think you're still playing the blame game.
- [ ] Stick to your request. You can acknowledge your spouse's retort ("Well, you always leave your dirty dishes in the sink.") with a simple, "Thank you for pointing that out. I am willing to talk with you about that. Could we finish with my request before we get to yours?"

Hopefully your spouse will realize that you are willing to address his/her concerns also and will allow you to continue. At first this will seem awkward and scripted. You can preface your talk by explaining that you read about a technique that you think will help you avoid blaming, and allow you to talk to your spouse in a more helpful manner.

Give yourself a break when you do this. It takes time and practice to apply new skills to your relationship before they become natural.

Affirmation: I keep in mind that it's all small stuff. I honor my relationship by focusing on what matters the most: loving each other.

63. Express your point of view and then let go of the need to have your spouse do what you think s/he should do.

If you have ever given advice, whether it was requested or unsolicited, you may have become invested in making sure your advice was followed. This often creates problems for you and the person you have given advice to.

Here's an example:

Jim has been working for a long time without a raise. His wife, Claire, tells him he should ask the boss to raise his salary. This is an example of unsolicited advice.

In a similar scenario, Jim has been trying to figure out the best way to approach the boss to ask for a raise. He asks for Claire's opinion, so they brainstorm together. In this case, he has asked for his wife's advice and help with some problem-solving.

Let's say that in both scenarios, Claire becomes so invested in her advice that every day after work she asks Jim whether he has talked to the boss yet. Claire may be excited about his getting a raise or maybe she is stressed out about the household finances. Whatever the reason, Claire is now even more invested in finding out if Jim took her advice.

When Jim tells her he hasn't talked to the boss, Claire begins to criticize him or nag him to hurry up and do it. What was once Jim's responsibility has now become Claire's self-appointed "job" to "make" him do what she advised him to do. As a result, Jim starts to feel resentful of what he considers Claire's meddling in his business. He doesn't want to talk to her about it.

Claire starts to feel some self-righteous indignation, saying things like, "Why did you even ask me if you weren't going to follow my advice?" Claire believes that she has some ownership in Jim's decision just because she gave him an opinion.

Action step:

If you believe that your spouse should do what you say just because you want her/him to, ask yourself these questions:

- ☐ Why does anyone have to follow my advice just because s/he asked for it? Or even if s/he didn't ask for it?
- ☐ If you still believe that your spouse should follow your advice, why should that be? According to what rule?

Advice, whether asked for or unsolicited, is just advice. If you start to feel overly invested in your spouse's decisions, ask yourself why you are doing this. If you feel strongly about a particular outcome, talk with your spouse about how you feel. You can make a request for what you want. However, avoid telling your spouse how s/he should act. All you can do is give your spouse information. **What s/he does with that information is not up to you.**

Affirmation: I express my point of view and let go of the need to have my spouse do what I think s/he should do.

> **64. If you make a decision that you think is sound, let go of the need for your spouse to agree with you.**

Jerry and Suzanne have been married for 21 years and they have teenage children. Their parenting styles differ, as is common with many of my clients. Sometimes they have some pretty intense disagreements about the "right" way to parent their children.

Jerry believes that all three of their children should be treated exactly the same and given the same rewards and punishments. Suzanne thinks that each child is different, learns differently, responds differently to discipline, and therefore has a tailored approach for each child.

Suzanne tends to be more permissive while Jerry is stricter. Often the conflicts revolve around Jerry complaining that he is the "bad guy" while Suzanne gets to be the "fun parent."

Their oldest son Ben, a freshman in high school, whom Suzanne sees as very responsible, has been doing his homework this school year without supervision. The younger children still sit at the dining room table together and do their homework with her (or Jerry's) supervision and show their parents their completed work.

Because Suzanne has decided that she trusts their eldest son, Ben, she has allowed him to do his homework in his room. She and Ben have agreed that Ben can keep this up as long he maintains good grades. Suzanne sees this as a reward for responsible behavior, and also a way to help her son begin to take personal responsibility for his own behavior without the need for her to constantly look over his shoulder.

Jerry, on the other hand, doesn't agree with Suzanne's parenting style in this case, so he and Suzanne argue. Jerry's way to solve the problem is to nag Ben about his homework and tell him to come to the table to get it done. In so doing, Jerry is effectively negating Suzanne's parenting decision.

It doesn't just end there. Suzanne thinks Jerry doesn't trust her decisions and Jerry believes that since Suzanne won't do the "right" thing (which essentially means doing what Jerry thinks is right) he has to take up the slack and do it himself.

Your spouse is not going to agree with you all the time. Sometimes conflicts escalate when you disagree about the "right" way to do something. Sometimes the spouse who argues longer and louder "wins," but in the end winning results in other problems:

- ☐ Resentment, anger, and bitterness
- ☐ Passive-aggressive behavior
- ☐ Sarcasm often followed by "I was just joking" or "you have no sense of humor"
- ☐ Snide comments in front of friends, family, or even the children
- ☐ Sneakiness (I'll keep doing it my way, but I won't do it in front of my disapproving spouse.)
- ☐ Defiance (I don't care what you think; I'm doing it my way.)
- ☐ Martyr behavior (I have to do everything around here if it's to be done right or done at all.)

It's human nature to want to be right and to want others to acknowledge that you are right. This is the source of many unresolved arguments. It involves unnecessary explaining and defending in an attempt to get another human to agree with you. Sometimes this comes from a need to please others or to convince yourself that you're doing the right thing.

Even if this is a long-standing behavior, you can learn new ways of relating. If you're willing to apply new behaviors, you can make a great difference in your interactions.

Action step:

In the case of Jerry and Suzanne, I agree that either parenting method is fine. The problem is that they had a power struggle going over **which way** was right. Ideally both parents would be onboard with a particular parenting strategy. However, both parents have a right to do what they believe is best, and most of the time neither way is "wrong".

If your usual pattern when your spouse challenges your decisions is to explain, get defensive, and lash out, step back and reevaluate. If you are certain that your decision is the right one for you, be confident. If you are dealing with similar arguments over how to raise your children (or anything in which the two of you do not see eye to eye), here are some things to consider:

- ☐ You are not going to agree with your spouse's parenting method one hundred percent. Ever. As long as what your spouse is doing is not illegal, immoral, unethical, dangerous, or violent, you will do better to accept that you have different **preferences** in how you relate to your children.
- ☐ If you disagree with your spouse's method, decide to trust that your spouse has your children's best interest at heart.
- ☐ If you believe that your way of dealing with your children is acceptable and proper, you do not have to defend your position.
- ☐ Often defending yourself leads to more arguing. If your spouse is questioning your parenting methods, it's all right to say, "I hear what you are saying. I am confident that I am doing the right thing. I appreciate your perspective; however, I am going to continue to do it this way."
- ☐ You do not need to explain or defend. You do not need to tell your spouse, "Why don't you trust me?" or even "You should trust me." You could decide to say, "I wish you would trust me" or "I would love to have your support" in a very gentle voice.
- ☐ If, in the end, your spouse still decides to go over your head and do it the "right" way (according to your spouse's way of thinking), let it go. In the case of Suzanne and Jerry, if Jerry insists that Ben sit at the table to do his homework, Suzanne cannot change Jerry's mind, but she can decide to let it go, knowing that Jerry has taken over the task in the manner he sees fit. When it is Suzanne's turn to be in charge of the homework, she can allow Ben to do his homework on his own. She would do well to let Jerry know that she is doing this. She will not help the situation if she goes behind Jerry's back and makes a secret agreement with their son.

- ☐ If Jerry complains that Suzanne is "making" him work extra hard, Suzanne can respond with, "If you choose to have Ben sit at the table and check his homework, that is fine." If Suzanne wants to say more, she can add, "I trust Ben and I know he will take personal responsibility for doing his homework." Only Jerry can choose his behavior.

As you read these ideas, keep in mind that they can apply to any subject in which you do not agree, not just in the area of childrearing.

Affirmation: I trust my judgment and I make sound decisions. I let go of the need for my spouse to agree with my decisions.

Compassion:

Walk a Mile in Your Spouse's Shoes

"A relationship is essentially the result of two sets of energies combining. If one of your energies changes, the result has to change also. Your primary responsibility is thus to maintain your energy."
Mark Semple, Successful Together Coaching

> **65. Take a walk in your spouse's shoes for a day and see what you learn.**

Taking the time to listen carefully and learn more about how your spouse sees the world is an eye-opening experience. Although you can never fully understand what your spouse has been through and what your spouse is thinking and feeling, you can come closer to relating when you take the time to see things from your spouse's perspective.

One of Stephen Covey's Seven Habits of Highly Effective People is "seek first to understand." The more you seek to understand, the better your connection to your spouse will be.

Action step:

The next time you have the urge to make a hasty judgment about your spouse, pause. Do this instead:

- ☐ Spend some time thinking about what it must be like to be your spouse. Write your thoughts in your journal. You will not know everything; that's not the point of this exercise. Your job is to reflect on what it must be like as best as you can from your perspective.
- ☐ Say these refreshing words, "Tell me more." When your spouse says something confusing or that gets under your skin, you can avoid conflict by asking for clarification with these three words.
- ☐ If your spouse says something that you don't understand, acknowledge it. Say, "I don't understand. Would you say more about that?"

Affirmation: I am willing to learn more about my spouse's perspective. I seek to understand.

66. Do unto others as they need to be done unto.

My former supervisor and mentor, the late Eugene Brown, frequently mentioned his own version of the Golden Rule: "Do unto others as they need to be done unto." When you realize what this distinction means, you begin to understand how your behavior affects others. Just because you would like something done in a certain way, you realize that others may not be of the same mind.

For example, you may be someone who loves hugs. You want to hug everyone you meet. One day you meet someone who is painfully shy and who recoils when you try to hug her. Your first reaction may be to think something is wrong with her. After all, hugs are wonderful, right?

But as you realize that she needs to "be done unto" differently, you accept that how you want to be treated is not what everyone wants. You understand that you must respect your new friend's boundaries and you change your behavior toward her to fit her needs.

Action step:

- ☐ Take the time to learn how others need to be treated, rather than just using a "one size fits all" approach. This is especially important when striving to create a happy marriage.
- ☐ Create a time to talk with your spouse about how s/he needs to be treated, continuing to "seek first to understand."

Affirmation: I understand that just because I like something in a certain way, it doesn't mean that everyone does. I am mindful of and sensitive to the needs of others.

67. You and your spouse have two different brains, so you're going to see things differently.

Do you know anyone who agrees with you 100% of the time? I didn't think so. Even your closest, dearest friends don't always agree with you. They may not say it, but they sometimes think differently than you do. Actually, it's probably a good thing when people do not agree with you; it allows you to learn something from another person's perspective, giving you food for thought even if you don't change your mind.

If you were married to someone who agreed with you all the time, it would start to feel a little creepy, as if you had married a Stepford wife. It may feed your ego at first, but eventually you would get bored and possibly feel contemptuous of your spouse.

An interesting part of being married is the different perspectives you and your spouse bring to your relationship. The two of you do not always think alike, so you will see things differently, which allows you both to learn things you may not have thought about previously.

Action step:

Sometimes when you and your spouse clash, even mildly, you may tend to see it as a big deal and get worked up over it. Try this instead: when you and your spouse see things differently, think about how you would act if your best friend and you did not see eye to eye.

- ☐ Do you and your best friend argue and yell at each other?
- ☐ Do you laugh it off and accept that the two of you are allowed your own opinions?
- ☐ Ask yourself how you can apply this same behavior to your disagreements with your spouse, and then do it.

Affirmation: I see things differently than my spouse sometimes and that is perfectly all right.

68. Men and women speak different languages. Learning the language of your spouse creates a strong connection.

If you have ever taken your dog to obedience school, one of the things you learn quickly is that often the problems that exist between you and your dog have little to do with the dog and more to do with you.

Dog trainers call this "handler error." Your dog wants to please you; that's the nature of dogs. They are extremely intelligent animals and they strive to learn your language to create that bond that makes them "man's best friend."

But dogs are not humans. Dogs do dog behaviors. They don't do them to make you mad or to get back at you. They do these dog behaviors because they are dogs. The more you understand about why dogs do what they do, the more enriching and rewarding your relationship with your canine companion will be. Your job is to learn your dog's "language" so that you can relate to him in a meaningful way.

You're probably scratching your head and wondering what this has to do with marriage. Stay with me, because this will blow you away. Men and women, who are in a sense, human animals, have different languages. Some of this is a result of biology and some is the result of socialization.

Because of these differences and your lack of awareness about them, you may often believe your spouse is just plain crazy. Your wife isn't crazy; she's just talking as women do. Likewise, your husband is not insane; he's just speaking the language of men.

You may even wonder why men can't just be more like women or vice versa. Ah, but then where's the fun? Just as learning as much about your canine companion can help you create a strong, loving bond with your furry friend Buster, learning as much as you can about your spouse's language will help you create the happy marriage you desire.

Action step:

- ☐ The next time you find yourself thinking, "My spouse must be crazy," stop and ask for clarification. You can say something like, "Honey, when you say that, I don't know what you mean. Can you explain it to me?"
- ☐ Saying, "I don't understand. Can you tell me more?" will also work.
- ☐ Thank your spouse for the explanation, even if you are still confused in the end. You can always ask for more clarification.
- ☐ Remember that learning your spouse's language will take some time. Be kind to yourself and to each other as you learn.

Affirmation: I enjoy the differences between me and my spouse. I strive to understand my spouse's language to create a strong bond between us.

> **69. Sometimes panic looks like anger. Strive to remain calm when your partner looks angry but is possibly scared.**

I recall an incident with Al in which we were arguing. I cannot remember what we were arguing about, but what I do remember is a sudden realization about Al's behavior. I knew he looked angry. He had all the signs of anger: the visible tension in his body, his raised voice, his tone, and facial features of anger. Yet, I realized something else and it stopped me in my tracks:

Al was panicking. As I made this connection, I was able to step back and reassess the situation with this new knowledge. I was able to feel compassion for my husband instead of anger toward him. Once I understood this new information, I was able to drop my defensive behavior. I was able to respond to him with kindness and compassion.

Can you relate? If so, here is your action step.

Action step:

- ☐ When you notice your spouse looks angry and sounds angry, instead of immediately jumping into conflict, pause and ask yourself whether s/he might be panicking. A word of caution: it will probably not be helpful to ask, "Honey, are you panicking?"
- ☐ If you can maintain your presence of mind, ask this soothing question: "What can I do to help?" Even if your spouse growls at you in response, you will have avoided engaging in a battle. You will have resisted fanning the flames.

Affirmation: I choose to see my spouse through loving eyes, even when we are in conflict.

Passion:

Keep the Fire Burning Brightly

"Marriage is not just spiritual communion and passionate embraces; marriage is also three meals a day, sharing the workload and remembering to carry out the trash." Dr. Joyce Brothers

> **70. Daily appreciation of the little things your spouse does goes a long way to create goodwill in your marriage.**

I have read that we need appreciation more than we need love. Whether this is true, I don't know, but I do know that appreciation is powerful. When my husband tells me, "Thank you for doing the dishes," even though I do them every day, I still feel good that he noticed and took the time to acknowledge me. In turn, I thank my husband for the things he does regularly, reciprocating the appreciation.

Action step:

Look for simple things your spouse does that you can express appreciation for. Show appreciation verbally and through written notes. Practice seeking things to appreciate and you will find plenty more.

Here are some examples:

- ☐ Washing the car
- ☐ Those courtesy calls to say s/he'll be home soon
- ☐ Planning your social events
- ☐ Calling from the store to see if you need anything
- ☐ Taking care of the bill payments
- ☐ Bringing home pizza so you don't have to cook
- ☐ Putting away the groceries after you brought them home
- ☐ Giving you that unexpected, and sorely needed, neck massage
- ☐ Maintaining the car
- ☐ Making the bed
- ☐ Getting the children in bed early so you can have some grown up time
- ☐ Always making sure the house is stocked with essentials
- ☐ That morning kiss before work

Affirmation: I focus on what I appreciate about my spouse daily.

> **71. Handle your marriage the way you would handle a newborn baby, carefully. It is a treasure.**

Do you find yourself neglecting your spouse? Do other priorities take over, leaving you with little time and energy to devote to your marriage? Maybe you've convinced yourself that you "must" do these other things. After all, the bills must be paid, the children must be fed, and many other people and activities demand your time.

Think about this: your marriage is the foundation of your family. Keep it strong and healthy by attending to it. You and your spouse are living examples for your children of how to create a successful relationship. What message do you want to give to your children about how to create a loving marriage?

Action step:

> ☐ Do you say "yes" when you would rather say no? Sometimes you take on too many activities that take you away from your marriage and family. Practice saying a gentle "no" like this:
>
> "I really appreciate you asking me and I wish I could do it but I can't." You don't have to offer an explanation. That would water down your statement. Smile and repeat yourself if the person asking you to do something doesn't take "no" for an answer.

Affirmation: I value my marriage and I make time for my spouse and me to spend together regularly.

72. It's hard to be sexually intimate with the one you love when you are holding onto bitterness and resentment.

Some people need to see a doctor about their low sex drive or other sexual problems in their marriage. I always recommend that my clients rule out anything physical when dealing with sexual problems. Sometimes the medication you are taking or other health problems can block normal, healthy sexual expression.

Some people have had sexually traumatic experiences in childhood or adulthood that have left them scarred, making it difficult to have a healthy expression of sexuality in their marriage. Those who have experienced sexual abuse as children or sexual violence such as rape as adults often benefit from therapy and support groups to address the impact of those traumas and to help them cope and recover.

For many couples stress is the culprit. Well, not stress itself, but your reaction to it or your inability to deal with stress. It could be the stress of managing work, home, children, and many other people and appointments that take up your time each day.

Most importantly, unresolved anger, bitterness, and resentment will leave you feeling anything but sexually attracted to your spouse. I find that this is often the case with many of my clients.

Often the woman will be the first to shut down sexually when she feels badly toward her husband, but not always. Some men are able to be sexual regardless of the climate of the relationship, but many shut down sexually just as many women do.

Sexual intimacy is very important when striving for a healthy, successful relationship. If you are having difficulty in this area of your life, it is hard to "just feel better and just do it." Anger and resentment take up a lot of emotional energy. A lot of energy is being siphoned away from your expression of sexual feelings. When you feel good about each other and toward each other, your natural feelings of attraction make it easy to be intimate.

If you are doing the Seven Deadly Habits to each other (criticizing, blaming, complaining, nagging, threatening, punishing, and rewarding/bribing to control) you are unlikely to feel sexually attracted to each other. You are more likely to be stuck in resentment, anger, and blame. It's hard to feel vulnerable (and sexual intimacy definitely requires vulnerability) when you are trying to control each other by using the Seven Deadly Habits.

Action step:

If you and your spouse are avoiding intimacy, do your homework to find out what is standing in the way of expressing your sexual feelings toward each other. Examining your interactions and feelings toward each other is a good place to start.

- ☐ Which of the Seven Deadly Habits are you doing that are creating distance in your marriage? Be honest with yourself as you acknowledge how you may be contributing to the difficulties. Write your insights in your journal.
- ☐ What stressors are you faced with lately?
- ☐ How are you dealing with the stress? List both helpful and not so helpful things you are doing.
- ☐ What plan can you make to reduce the stress or deal with it more effectively?
- ☐ Write out any feelings of anger, bitterness, and resentment that you have been holding onto that may contribute to your lack of desire for your spouse.
- ☐ Ask yourself which of these feelings you can let go of now. You may be holding onto old feelings that no longer have any value to you. Ask yourself whether they are benefiting you and your spouse.

Affirmation: I now let go of the anger and resentment that is standing in the way of being close to my spouse. I am working toward creating emotional and physical intimacy in my marriage.

73. Reignite the passion in your marriage by asking for what you want and expressing appreciation for what you like.

Maybe your marriage has fallen into a predictable routine and you wonder where the love has gone. You may lament that your husband never brings you flowers anymore or that he doesn't surprise you by taking you special places like he used to when you were first in love. Maybe the demands of motherhood have reduced your wife's availability for couple time, or even her energy level for sexual intimacy.

I believe that if you do not start by addressing the way you treat each other daily, your love life will remain, well, lifeless. If you want to bring back the loving feelings that helped you to fall in love with your spouse, begin by examining how you interact with each other. The way you express yourself makes a huge difference.

Here are some ineffective ways to attempt to get your needs met:

Criticism/comparison:
Wife: You never do anything romantic anymore; why can't you be more like Ana's husband?
Husband: What's wrong with you? You used to want to have sex all the time. Now I have to beg for it.

Hints:
Husband: My ex used to be ready for sex whenever I wanted it.
Wife: Sarah's husband took her to their favorite restaurant this weekend and they danced until the place closed.

Complaints:
Wife: You never bring me flowers anymore.
Husband: You never initiate sex anymore.

Nagging:
Husband: I keep asking you to be more open to new things in bed, but you keep turning me down.
Wife: I've asked you over and over to do something romantic with me and you never do.

Threatening/punishing:
Wife: If you don't remember my birthday this year, I won't have sex with you for a month.
Husband: If you won't do something about our lack of passion, I'll find someone who will.

If you look at these statements, they are all attempts to get your spouse to change his/her present behavior by cajoling, directly or indirectly. Most people do not respond to this kind of manipulation with positive, loving feelings. Instead, the usual outcome is resentment and defensiveness. Not a great way to get your needs met, right?

If you want to get your needs met and create good feelings in the process, use another approach.

Action step for women:

- ☐ Instead of hinting, be direct. If you want to go out dancing, tell your husband what you want. Offer to find a place to go and set a date. "But that's not romantic," you say. Why not? Why can't it be? You want him to initiate. If you have been direct and he has not initiated, plan your romantic outing and stop whining about it!
- ☐ If he is willing and you are able to tell him that you would love to be surprised, that's wonderful. You are indeed fortunate. But expecting him to read your mind and create a surprise will leave you disappointed. Tell him that you want him to surprise you, and then wait for it without nagging.
- ☐ If you want your distracted husband to remember your birthday, you may need to do some planning, rather than expecting him to remember. Put it on his calendar; write him reminders; plan a date with him.
- ☐ Appreciate instead of criticize: "I love it when you bring me flowers" is a great start. In fact, if you get nothing else out of this article, remember that a healthy dose of appreciation can put the passion back into your marriage. When your husband feels appreciated, he will reciprocate. You'll feel better too.

Action step for men:

- ☐ Watch a feel good movie or a romantic comedy with her.
- ☐ Recall the things you did when you were first together. How did you treat her back then? What behaviors can you bring back into your present interactions with your wife?
- ☐ Sit with your wife and have a talk about what each of you are willing to do, and interested in trying out, to reignite the passion.
- ☐ Learn all you can about how a woman needs to be treated so that she can feel open to being intimate.

Affirmation: I take responsibility for keeping the passion thriving in my marriage. I ask for what I need and am receptive to my spouse's needs.

> **74. Date night is especially important if you have small children.**

My sister Kimberly has three young children. She and her husband, Trey, are dedicated to being conscientious parents and are very involved in their children's activities, yet they understand the importance of Grown Up Time. I've always admired their commitment to their time with each other.

Our parents had a similar pattern. They left us with trustworthy sitters so that they could have some time together on a regular basis. Whether you are new parents, parents with teens, parents with grown and flown children, or you have no children at all, regular date nights with your spouse are important.

You may think that you do not have time or money to do this. You can still create date nights that allow you and your spouse to reconnect with each other. Don't let the thought that you don't have the time or money to do this stop you. Your marriage depends on your willingness to make couple time a priority on a regular basis.

Action step:

The key to successful date nights, especially when your lives are hectic, is to be flexible. Here are some ideas to get you started:

- ☐ Schedule your date nights for a certain night of the week. Any day will do as long as it works for both of you. Be flexible if you're not able to have your date on the night you had originally planned.
- ☐ A date can be elaborate or incredibly simple. Some date nights may be dinner and a movie. Others may be a bottle of wine and a rented movie at home after putting the children to bed.
- ☐ Holiday dates: just because Valentine's Day, your anniversary, or birthdays fall on a certain date on the calendar, you don't have to be a slave to that date. If another day of the week works better to celebrate, do it then.

Affirmation: I value my grown up time with my spouse and I treasure our date nights.

> **75. Keeping a familiar routine for your children allows you and your spouse to have Grown Up Time together in the evening.**

I've always been impressed with the teamwork I've witnessed between my sister Kimberly and Trey. They have a routine that works for them. Once their three young children have finished dinner, both parents work together to get them ready for bed, which includes bathing, brushing teeth, and reading a book to them.

Working together, they have their children in bed by 8:00 pm. This gives my sister and Trey time to spend with each other before they retire for the night.

My parents made sure they had us children to bed early. As a child I was usually mad, especially during daylight savings time, because it was still light out when we went to bed. My mom would tell us we didn't have to go to bed, but we had to stay in our rooms. As an adult, I understand what my parents were doing, though I didn't like it as a child!

It is so important to set boundaries with your children so that you and your spouse can have some uninterrupted time together. Keeping a reasonable bedtime for your children is a win in at least two ways: it allows you to insure that they get enough sleep and it gives you the grown up time you and your spouse need.

Action step:

If you have not set some workable routines with your children, this may be harder for you. Seek help with this important job if you need it. I encourage you to take some parenting classes that are appropriate for your children's age level.

- ☐ If you have children, begin to set boundaries around your children's bedtime to allow you and your spouse to have some time together in the evening.
- ☐ Even if you do not have children, take some time each evening to reconnect with your spouse in a meaningful way. It doesn't have to be anything elaborate. It can be sitting together for dinner and talking about your day, your weekend plans, or anything else that is interesting or important. Even playing a game together can be fun and good "couple time."

Affirmation: I value spending time with my spouse. I take the time to reconnect with my spouse each evening.

Conflict Resolution:

Creating Harmony at Home

"When you plant lettuce, if it does not grow well, you don't blame the lettuce...Yet if we have problems with our friends or family, we blame the other person...Blaming has no positive effect at all, nor does trying to persuade using reason and argument. That is my experience. No blame, no reasoning, no argument, just understanding. If you understand, and you show that you understand, you can love, and the situation will change." Thich Nhat Hanh

76. How badly do you want to win the argument? Enough to lose the relationship?

Dr. Glasser asks, "Which is more important, winning the argument or keeping the relationship?" If your ego is getting in the way of loving your spouse, it's time to examine your beliefs about arguing.

"But I'm right!" What good does it do to be right when you are all alone and there is no one left to argue with about how right you are? If being right is a priority for you, your relationship with the one you love is taking a back seat to your ego.

The problem with being right in a relationship is that it really doesn't matter. Being right matters when you take a test, you travel to a destination and you need to take the correct road, or you are solving a problem.

Being "right" in your relationship can cause some serious arguing, especially if both of you think you are right. "This is how we always did it in my family" doesn't cut it. It only means you have a **preference** for the way things are done, not that your way is the right way or the only way.

Action steps:

- ☐ The next time you feel the need to prove your "rightness," ask yourself: would I rather be right or in harmony with the one I love?
- ☐ Remember that there are many ways to do something and your way is your preference, not the only right way to do something.
- ☐ Remember that the only time when being right is extremely important is when you know your life or someone else's life is in danger (the house is on fire, your car is about to plunge over the edge of a cliff, sword-wielding ninjas have just broken through the roof of the restaurant where you're eating...stuff like that). Even then you don't waste time saying, "I told you so." You focus your energy on getting to safety!

Affirmation: I now allow myself to let go of the need to be right. I am at peace and I prefer closeness to with my spouse over "rightness."

77. When you hurt the one you love, be quick to apologize.

Conflicts are an unavoidable part of relationships; arguments are optional. You can decide how to manage them and you can learn to pick your battles. But what happens when they are over? Do you apologize? Do you simmer in anger for a few days, and then pretend nothing happened?

What if you were not at fault for the argument? Are you sure? Before you decide that you were the injured party and your spouse is the villain, think about it. You may not have started the conflict, but you engaged in it. You probably said hurtful things during the argument.

What can you apologize for?

If you allow yourself to hear the hurt (and often panic) in your spouse's angry rant, you may learn something. If you listen and seek to understand, you can find something to apologize for.

Why should you apologize?

A heart felt apology clears the air. It rebuilds trust. It allows the two of you to get a fresh start. But it must be sincere or it won't work. Also, an apology will help you feel better. It is sometimes hard to do, especially if you are still holding onto anger. If you can see past the anger and decide that your relationship is more important than the conflict, you can apologize easier. You value your relationship above any differences you and your spouse are having.

What if your spouse does not accept your apology?

Don't sweat it. In this case, your spouse is not ready to let go of the hurt yet. It doesn't make your apology invalid. It simply means your spouse is not in the same place you are. You offered the olive branch and that is a great step in the right direction. Now your job is to "act as if" things are good between you. You don't have to go overboard to placate your spouse. Just be the calm, pleasant person you usually are, treating your spouse with the dignity and respect you would like in return.

Action step:

In every conflict there is something you can apologize for, even if it's as simple as the fact that you allowed the conflict to go on and you participated in it.

- ☐ Figure out how you can clear the air and offer your own olive branch by asking yourself, "What can I apologize for?"
- ☐ Offer your apology; be gracious even if your spouse is not acting similarly, then move on, away from the argument.

Affirmation: I understand the value of apologizing. I have no need to keep my guard up. I apologize for my contribution to the conflict.

> **78. Reflective listening is a gift you give to each other to understand on a deeper level.**

"The first duty of love is to listen." Paul Tillich

If you have felt your spouse has listened to you actively, with all her/his energy, you know what a wonderful gift it is.

This next exercise is not meant to resolve conflict necessarily (although it can), but rather to get you off the Merry-Go-Round of One-Upmanship. It stops your pattern of being more eager to defend yourself against what you interpret as attacks than to listen to the deeper meaning.

This exercise also helps you speak your thoughts and feelings in such a way that promotes compassion instead of outrage and retaliation, as is the pattern with many couples. It is hard for couples in a negative pattern to lower their defensive shields long enough to hear raw emotional pain that may be coming from their loved one. It may also be hard to be honest enough to allow those "not so nice" thoughts to come out when a pattern of verbal sword fighting has been the norm for too long.

Before you and your spouse get started, think about the outcome you desire. This is mostly about seeking to understand, so think about that as a possible outcome. Calm, easy discussion could be another outcome.

Remember that this exercise is much more effective when you and your spouse remain in the adult role. Leave the ego at the door. You are with a friend and there is no need to defend yourself. You are safe.

Spouse 1 is the Sender: Send a **short, simple message** using assertive language:

- ☐ For example: "I feel sad/hurt/disappointed when you don't call me during your lunch break" or "I feel like you don't care about me, like I'm not important."
- ☐ Ask for what you want: I would like for you to call me during your break at least 3 times a week.

Spouse 2 has a simple job at this point (no interpreting meaning or defending yourself, just tell your spouse what you heard):

- ☐ For example: "What I hear you saying is that you feel sad/hurt/disappointed when I don't call you during my lunch break. You feel like I don't care about you and you feel unimportant. You would like for me to call you during my break at least 3 times a week."
- ☐ Follow up with, "Did I get it right?" Usually you are paraphrasing and will not always catch everything. This is your spouse's opportunity to tell you what you might have missed or to say, "Yes, you got it."
- ☐ Next, you say the three magic words, "Tell me more."

One of the greatest gifts you can give your spouse is listening fully. When you do not understand something, ask for clarification. "I don't understand the part about _____. Could you explain that a bit more?" will work.

Next Spouse 2, the Receiver, has the opportunity to walk a mile in the shoes of Spouse 1. This is to help Spouse 1 feel understood and to help Spouse 2 to empathize.

- ☐ This is what I got from what you have told me _____.
- ☐ I can see how my behavior affects you when I _____.
- ☐ I take responsibility for _____.

☐ This is what I am able/willing to do _____.
(This part may require some negotiating, especially if the request for change is not amenable to Spouse 1)

Once Spouse 1 is done, you can switch roles and do this again if you wish.

Although you will never fully understand another person's thoughts, feelings, and motivations, you can come closer to understanding by being open to hearing him/her out instead of immediately rushing to defend yourself.

Defensiveness shuts down communication. It says that you are only interested in making sure you are understood and that your spouse does or says things in such a way that you want. Remember that one of Stephen Covey's Seven Habits of Highly Effective People is "Seek first to understand, then to be understood."

The more time you spend seeking to understand your spouse, rather than attempting to force your spouse to understand you first, the less time you will spend arguing and defending yourself against an imaginary enemy.

It is very important to steer clear of the destructive behaviors that tear down communication, especially during this exercise. You are deciding to trust each other as you willingly let down your guard and speak with your heart.

Be careful to avoid doing anything that will damage that trust. Some behaviors that shut down communication are:

- ☐ Criticizing
- ☐ Blaming
- ☐ Judging
- ☐ Interpreting
- ☐ Interrupting
- ☐ Sarcasm
- ☐ Mind-reading
- ☐ Using the past as a way to get back at each other
- ☐ Denying/negating/defending while you are in listening mode, but also when you are the one who is sharing your thoughts and feelings

If at all possible, this exercise is best done with a mediator, such as a therapist or a relationship coach (or a trusted family member or friend). It is difficult to do unless both of you are willing to exercise self-control. After you have begun to feel comfortable with this exercise, you will be able to do it without a mediator.

Affirmation: I listen actively and with my whole being to my spouse.

79. Avoid looking at the one you love with the "the look that kills."

Although I agree that eye contact is important, I think there are times when looking your spouse in the eye can cause more harm than good. If you are angry and you are familiar with the expression "If looks could kill" you don't want that kind of look to be etched into your spouse's mind. Instead, reserve your looks of love for your spouse.

Conflicts are going to happen just as surely as the sun sets in the west. It's good to be prepared with a bunch of different tools in your Conflict Resolution Toolbox to help you deal with the conflicts effectively.

Arguing does not have to degenerate into schoolyard behavior, saying hurtful things that will be remembered long after the reason for the argument is forgotten. This kind of mud-slinging slowly strangles the love you have for each other until you and your spouse become nothing more than verbal sparring partners.

Over the years I have recommended some pretty strange, unconventional, and sometimes downright silly ways to argue. If you are willing to experiment with some of these, you may find it harder to argue in the same way you always do. Sometimes the sillier it sounds, the more effective it is.

The purpose of the following action step is to help you break your usual arguing pattern and detour you from the downward negative spiral that often follows. This helps you step back and think instead of shooting off the first thing on your mind, which is often unhelpful and many times something you regret saying later.

Action step:

You are free to argue, but here are some things you must do (if you choose to do these exercises) before you begin your argument. Note: I have used some of these techniques with good results myself. Remember, everyone has conflicts in their marriage, even therapists and relationship coaches!

- ☐ **Argue for short periods of time.** Set a timer for 10 minutes. When the timer goes off, stop the argument. Take a break for an hour, then come back and argue for 10 more minutes. Hopefully, during your hour break, you have had time to think through things. This can help you gain another perspective and perhaps help the two of you come up with a solution.
- ☐ **Argue in a different room of the house.** If you always argue in the bedroom, argue in the living room instead (provided that it is a private space). If you always argue inside, argue in the garage (this will help you keep your voices down unless you want the neighbors to hear, which I hope you do not).
- ☐ **Argue at a different time of day.** If you tend to argue right when you come home from work, wait until after dinner.
- ☐ **Argue back to back.** Place two chairs back to back in a private space. The rationale for doing this is that when you cannot see the angry gestures and facial expressions, you cut off that source of pain and distraction immediately. Also, since you cannot see the person you are arguing with you must focus more on listening to what your spouse is saying.
- ☐ **Switch sides and argue from your spouse's point of view.** This is probably one of those exercises you will do when you are not in serious conflict. It's hard to do and yet you can learn so much from it. Take on a minor bone of contention that you and your spouse have argued about regularly. Since you probably know your spouse's perspective very well, you have an opportunity to argue from that point of view. Argue with passion about it. This is not about getting sarcastic and belittling your spouse's perspective. It's about truly seeing it from "the other side" and arguing in favor of the outcome from your spouse's side.

- ☐ **Hold hands.** Sometimes when you gently hold the hand of the one you love, you find it is harder to argue loudly. Your voice may become softer and your tone less angry when you are doing something that is usually a sign of affection.
- ☐ **Put on formal clothes.** You can argue all you want once you dress yourself up as fancy as you can. Once you begin to focus on getting dressed to the nines you may begin to cool down. This can give you time to realize your argument is not worth it. Sometimes the silliness of arguing in a tuxedo and floor-length gown changes the atmosphere. Maybe you can find a reason to go out and do something fun when you are no longer inclined to argue.
- ☐ **Whisper.** I wouldn't recommend arguing in public, especially in a place where there is a need to whisper such as during a movie, while in a place of worship, or while watching your child perform in a school play. No, do this in the comfort of your own private space. Instead of talking in what often ends up being a harsh tone or a loud voice, whisper.
- ☐ **Argue on paper.** Pass notes to each other, just as you did when you were passing love notes in class many years ago. Arguing in this manner takes time. It gives you time to read each other's comments and respond. Remember to keep it clean. This is not the time to regress into your Child Role, writing nasty, sarcastic comments. Careful there! Stick to your point on paper and be as concise as you can in explaining why you think and feel as you do. Respond to each other's comments before writing your own comment. Often, in verbal arguments, listening goes out the window as you seek to be heard and to say your piece. This technique slows you down and allows you to think before responding.
- ☐ **Argue in Pig Latin.** This could get silly very quickly and laughter helps to dissolve anger, especially when you are both laughing about the same thing. If you don't know Pig Latin (which is quite fun, by the way) you can learn relatively quickly.

My husband's first language is Spanish and sometimes when we are in conflict I will deliberately switch to Spanish. Even though I am fluent in Spanish, it slows me down because I am not used to expressing myself while discussing conflict in my second language. I do it to convey my ideas to him in his first language and to give him an opportunity to speak in the language of his birth.

All of these tools require you to exercise self-control, which is often the first thing to be discarded when you start arguing.

**Just for Fun
A Word About Pig Latin:**

My parents inadvertently taught me Pig Latin when I was in elementary school. They wanted to say something without my understanding it, so they used Pig Latin. I figured it out pretty quickly and taught as many of my friends as I could. I didn't want to be left out and I figured I was doing a public service for my friends whose parents might have also been speaking this made up language.

Here's a quick example of Pig Latin: I-ay eak-spay ig-Pay atin-Lay. Take the first letter or first sound off the front of the word and speak the vowel part of it. Put the beginning letter, usually a consonant, behind and add an "ay" sound to it.

For example, my name, Michelle, would become ichelle-May. If the word has more than one consonant, like the word "string," it becomes ing-stray. If the word begins with a vowel, like the word "elevator," it simply becomes "elevator-ay."

Affirmation: I choose to slow down and learn new ways of relating to my spouse, and I choose to use these new skills when we are in conflict.

80. Boxers take a break every three minutes. Why not give your marriage a break when you are in conflict?

Time out. It's not just for children. Time out is a device used in sports to take a break, regroup, and plan a new strategy. If boxers get a break every three minutes, why not take a tip from them when you are arguing with your spouse?

Action step:

Here are some guidelines for using a Time Out. You can modify it to fit your situation, of course. First of all, introduce your spouse to the Time Out method when you are both calm. Shouting, "Time Out" during a heated argument will probably get you an odd look if your spouse has no idea what you are talking about.

Time out format:

- ☐ When the argument is getting heated, you may be concerned about saying or doing things that you will regret. This is a good time to ask for a time out. Tell your spouse, "I need a time out" or "I need a break."
- ☐ Refrain from telling your spouse, "You need a time out." Your spouse is not a child to put in a Time Out chair, even if it sometimes seems s/he acts like one!
- ☐ Remember that conflicts are uncomfortable. Discomfort is not a reason for a Time Out. Fear of losing self-control or when either of you have begun to "hit below the belt" (cursing, name-calling, rude comments, bringing up past arguments) are good reasons to call a Time Out.
- ☐ Please DO NOT use time out as a way to avoid dealing with something. Too many of my clients have decided that if they are uncomfortable with something their spouse has said they retreat under the "protection" of the Time Out.
- ☐ Once Time Out has been called, disengage. You may be tempted, but this is not the time to get in a parting shot, unless, of course, you want to make the situation worse. If that is the case, you really need to work on your conflict resolutions

skills! That behavior is your Child Role. Time out helps you stay in the Adult Role.

- [ ] Set a timer if you choose to. Synchronize your watches if you want to get fancy. However you do it, honor the hour and come back when it is done.
- [ ] Take one hour to do something physical. I strongly recommend that you stay near your home, but that you separate into different locations. Here are some ideas: take a walk around the neighborhood, do some exercise, run the vacuum cleaner, mop the floor. You get the idea.
- [ ] You do not have to spend your entire hour doing something physical, though it is important that you remain separated for the hour to give yourself time for your body to settle back down.
- [ ] Your autonomic nervous system is already revved up. You probably feel it in your body. Your adrenaline is pumping. Your heart beats faster and your muscles are tense. You feel a twisting in your gut. The reason for doing something physical is to help you to release some of the tension in your body in a healthy way.
- [ ] Avoid drinking alcohol or doing drugs. If you have some calming herbal tea that won't knock you out, you could drink that, or slowly sip a glass of water.
- [ ] You can also meditate, do yoga, pray, or do whatever other calming activities you can think of. Calming music might also be helpful, but keep the volume low so that it benefits you and does not add stress to your spouse who may be in the next room.
- [ ] I encourage you to avoid driving during this time. Your "Brain on Anger" is not as impaired as your brain on alcohol or drugs, but you are not necessarily as safe and focused as you would be when you are calm.
- [ ] Avoid spending your hour thinking things like, "What a jerk. How dare s/he treat me this way? Why did I ever agree to get married? Nothing but trouble all the time." Recognize that these types of thoughts are going to pop up. That's normal. You can choose whether to linger there.

- ☐ **Your mental task during this time is to ask yourself, "How can I be a part of the solution?"**
- ☐ Next take a pen and paper and start writing everything you can think of to answer the question, "How can I be a part of the solution?" This is not the time to write out your spouse's faults unless you want to continue the fight. This is the time to acknowledge how you are contributing to the problem. (Ouch! That's tough. Of course it is. But you want to make things work, right?)
- ☐ Remember the Seven Deadly Habits of External Control? Criticizing, blaming, nagging, complaining, threatening, punishing, and rewarding/bribing? Write which of these habits you are using during this conflict. Be honest with yourself. The more willing you are to acknowledge your part in the conflict the more headway you will make in resolving it.
- ☐ Ask yourself this question: "What am I willing to do right now that I think will help resolve this conflict?" Remember the Seven Caring Habits? (Supporting, Encouraging, Listening, Accepting, Trusting, Respecting, and Negotiating Differences). Look at these and decide which to begin with to help you resolve the conflict.
- ☐ When you return to your spouse after the hour is done, take your list of ideas with you and discuss them.
- ☐ If you begin to revert to pointing fingers, agree to another break. If you are unable to come to some sort of resolution after two breaks, agree to let go of it until the following day.
- ☐ Schedule a time to talk the following day. Often if you can sleep on a problem, you feel differently about it in the morning. Sometimes putting the problem aside for a day helps you gain a fresh perspective.
- ☐ Honor your agreement to talk again the next day.
- ☐ If you find that you still cannot find a solution that works for you both, you may need to consider getting guidance from a relationship coach or marriage counselor.

Affirmation: I am learning and using new tools to be a part of the solution when conflicts arise.

Creating Your Very Own Happily Ever After

"A great marriage is not when the 'perfect couple' comes together. It is when an imperfect couple learns to enjoy their differences."
Dave Meurer, *Daze of Our Wives*

> **81. Write your own love story with generous helpings of appreciation, admiration, and gratitude.**

Sometimes you may overlook the **attitudes** that create an air of romance, and it's my job to remind you. What do I mean by attitudes? Your attitude toward your spouse is crucial for creating romance and all sorts of good feelings. Your love story begins with how you treat your spouse on a daily basis. When you and your spouse feel appreciated, you are more likely to want to snuggle, hug, and kiss and otherwise get busy doing sexy things with and to each other. The opposite is also true. If you feel unappreciated by your spouse, you won't feel all warm and fuzzy toward her/him.

How can you create an atmosphere of appreciation, admiration, and gratitude?

Keep in mind that often the less expensive route works just as well, and at times it actually works better. You've probably heard the expression "throwing money at the problem." If you are a man who brings your wife flowers and expensive jewelry after every fight, I hope you have a ton of money to do so. I would not want you to go into debt with this tactic.

My take on the flowers and jewelry after fights? It seems like you are buying your wife's affection instead of looking for a solution to the regular conflicts. There's nothing wrong with showing affection with gifts. But what I would want you to avoid is giving gifts to appease your spouse or soothe your guilty conscience. The danger is that the gift can come to represent a fight and may be seen negatively instead of as something to be treasured.

Instead of "make up" gifts and "make up" sex, strive to create an atmosphere in which both of you are excited to come home to be together after your day is done. Do this with regular doses of appreciation, admiration, and gratitude.

Appreciation: when you appreciate your spouse, you raise his/her value. You recognize your spouse's importance and hold him/her in high esteem. You cherish and treasure your spouse. Appreciation is a very loving thing to do, showing your spouse how much you value, esteem, and cherish her/him.

Admiration: when you admire your spouse, you see her/him with pleasure, wonder, and approval. When I think of admiration, I see a woman with her hands clasped and held to her face, gazing lovingly at her hero. This vivid image is a stereotype, yet it doesn't make the image any less powerful. Do you gaze lovingly at your spouse, seeing her/him with pleasure, wonder, and approval?

Gratitude: someone who is grateful is thankful and shows pleasure at what s/he has received. People show their gratitude through simple phrases like, "Thank you so much for..." or "I am so grateful for..." Why wait to show your gratitude only during Thanksgiving? Being grateful toward your spouse and expressing your gratitude regularly will definitely help your marriage thrive.

Action step:

- ☐ Create a page in your journal with the words Appreciation, Admiration, and Gratitude at the top. Use more pages if you need it.
- ☐ Spend about ten minutes brainstorming all the things you can come up with that you appreciate, admire, and are grateful for about your spouse. You can add more later. This is just to get you started.
- ☐ Refer to your list often, especially when the every day stresses make it hard to remember.
- ☐ Make a point to tell your spouse something on your list regularly. Doing this daily is ideal, but if you begin with three to four days a week, it's a start in the right direction.

Understand that the stressors of life may make it difficult to do this at the same enthusiastic level every single day. That's all right. The good thing about doing these things regularly is that when things are tough, you will have built up so much good will and good feelings that you are able to handle the stressful times better.

A reporter once challenged Zig Ziglar, saying that motivation doesn't last. Zig replied that neither does bathing, and that's why we recommend showering daily. Similarly, regular applications of appreciation, admiration, and gratitude are needed to allow your love to thrive.

Affirmation: I show regular appreciation, admiration, and gratitude to my spouse. It is becoming a habit for me.

As you work through these exercises and make the tools your own, you will be well on your way to creating your very own happily ever after. I know you can do it. I believe in you and I hope that your belief in yourself (and in your happy marriage) grows stronger every day!

"May laughter fall upon you like the rain, and blessings shine upon you like the sun. May joy always be stronger than the pain, and love embrace you when the day is done." Kim M. Baldwin

Recommended Reading

Berne, Eric, MD. *Games People Play.*

Burns, David D., MD. *The Feeling Good Handbook: Overcome Depression, Conquer Anxiety, and Enjoy Greater Intimacy.*

Chapman, Gary. *The 5 Love Languages: the Secret to Love that Lasts.*

Chapman, Gary, and Campbell, Ross. *The 5 Love Languages of Children.*

Cline, Foster, and Fay, Jim. *Parenting with Love & Logic.*

Cloke, Bill, PhD. *Happy Together: Creating a Lifetime of Connection, Commitment, and Intimacy.*

Doyle, Laura. *The Surrendered Wife: A Practical Guide to Finding Intimacy, Passion, and Peace with a Man.*

Ellis, Albert, PhD. *Anger: How to Live With and Without it*

Fisher, Helen, PhD. *Why We Love: The Nature and Chemistry of Romantic Love.*

Gil, Eliana. *Outgrowing the Pain: A Book For and About Adults Abused As Children.*

Glasser, William, MD. *For Parents and Teenagers: Dissolving the Barrier Between You and Your Teen*

Glasser, William, MD, and Glasser, Carleen. *Eight Lessons for a Happier Marriage*

Glasser, William, MD, and Glasser, Carleen. *Getting Together and Staying Together: Solving the Mystery of Marriage.*

Godek, Greg. *1001 Ways to be Romantic.*

Glover, Robert A., PhD. *No More Mr. Nice Guy: A Proven Plan for Getting What You Want in Love, Sex, and Life.*

Gottman, John M., PhD. *The Seven Principles for Making Marriage Work: A Practical Guide from the Country's Foremost Relationship Expert.*

Gottman, John M., PhD. *Why Marriages Succeed or Fail.*

Gray, John, PhD. *Mars and Venus in the Bedroom: a Guide to Lasting Romance and Passion.*

Gunther, Randi, PhD. *Relationship Saboteurs: Overcoming the Ten Behaviors That Undermine Love.*

Hay, Louise L. *You Can Heal Your Life.*

Hanh, Thich Nhat. *Anger: Wisdom For Cooling the Flame.*

Katie, Byron. *I Need Your Love—Is That True? How to Stop Seeking Love, Approval, and Appreciation and Start Finding Them Instead.*

Katie, Byron. *Question Your Thinking, Change the World: Quotations from Byron Katie.*

Leiberman, David J. *Make Peace with Anyone: Breakthrough Strategies to Quickly End Any Conflict, Feud, or Estrangement.*

O'Hanlon, Bill and Hudson, Pat. *Love is a Verb: How to Stop Analyzing Your Relationship & Start Making it Great.*

Oliver, Kim, LPC. *Secrets of Happy Couples: Loving Yourself, Your Partner, and Your Life.*

Pease, Allan and Pease, Barbara. *Why Men Don't Listen and Women Can't Read Maps: How We're Different and What to Do About It.*

Rosemond, John. *Parenting by the Book.*

Tannen, Deborah. *You Just Don't Understand: Women and Men in Conversation.*

Tannen, Deborah. *That's Not What I Meant!: How Conversational Style Makes or Breaks Relationships*

Tipping, Colin. *Radical Forgiveness.*

Waite, Linda J. and Gallagher, Maggie. *The Case For Marriage: Why Married People are Happier, Healthier, and Better off Financially.*

Weiner Davis, Michelle. *Divorce Busting: A Revolutionary and Rapid Program for Staying Together.*

Weiner Davis, Michelle. *The Sex-Starved Marriage: Boosting Your Marriage Libido.*

Creating Happily Ever After™:
Relating from the Heart™ Process

The Relating from the Heart™ Process, created by Michelle Vásquez, is a step-by-step method designed to help married women over 40 learn dynamic ways to relate at the heart level, and rekindle a sense of passion with the man in her life.

Through experiential methods you learn highly effective skills of compassionate listening, communication, and problem-solving by reconnecting with, and remembering the deep feelings, that led you to say "I do" to your husband. If you love your husband, but you're not "in love" with him, together we will work to rekindle the love that is not lost, but is simply asking to be remembered.

Find out how to attend in-person workshops and tele-classes with Michelle. Contact her at michelle@michellevasquez.com. **Take what you've learned in this book to the next level with the Relating from the Heart™ Process.**

www.ingramcontent.com/pod-product-compliance
Lightning Source LLC
Chambersburg PA
CBHW071454040426
42444CB00008B/1331